America's National Parks

A Photographic Guide through All 63 National Parks of the USA

Table of Contents

Acadia
Maine

Park History

For many years, the Wabanaki people inhabited the area now known as Acadia National Park. One of the earliest Europeans to arrive at this beautifully diverse land was French explorer Samuel de Champlain, who gave it the name Isles des Monts Deserts (islands of bare peaks) in 1604 because of its granite-domed mountains. In the late 1800s, it became a popular vacation destination of the East Coast elite, including families such as the Rockefellers, Carnegies, and Vanderbilts.

The formation of Acadia National Park is unique in that it was formed due to the dedication and donations of private citizens who wanted to preserve the natural beauty of the land. This effort was led by George B. Dorr, known as "the father of Acadia National Park," and Charles W. Elliot. John D. Rockefeller Jr. donated 11,000 acres and was instrumental in the development of the carriage roads. He constructed these roads on Mount Desert Island from 1913-1940 because he wanted to travel via horse and carriage without the disruption of automobiles. Today, the carriage roads are open to horses, bicyclists, and pedestrians.

In July 1916, Woodrow Wilson designated the area as Sieur de Monts National Monument. In 1919, when it became the first national park east of the Mississippi, the name was changed to Lafayette National Park. The park was officially named Acadia National Park in January 1929. Acadia is currently one of the top 10 most visited national parks in the country, with over 3 million visitors each year.

Park Features

One of the best ways to get a fantastic overview of Acadia National Park is by driving along Park Loop Road. The 27-mile road winds through some of the park's finest scenery as it passes trailheads, beaches, headlands, and magnificent views of Penobscot Bay. The road begins near Hulls Cove Visitor Center and includes several stops along the way for visitors to take photos and explore the area, which can stretch the drive out for a full day. One such stop is at Sieur de Monts, where visitors can view the Wild Gardens of Acadia. The lower Sand Beach parking lot starts the 1.4-mile moderate walking trail that follows the perimeter of the Great Head Peninsula, where granite steps lead down to Sand Beach and provide a view of the cliffs.

Park Loop Road continues on, leading to sites such as the inlet known as Thunder Hole. When the waves hit just right, this deep inlet with a submerged cavern can roar and shoot water 40 feet into the air. The Jordan Pond House, with its beautiful views, is also a wonderful place to stop for a snack before heading up the switchbacks leading to the top of Cadillac Mountain, which rises to 1,528 feet.

Ecosystem

Acadia National Park consists of diverse ecosystems, including forests, wetlands, ponds/lakes, and an intertidal region. Spruce and pitch pine forests cover the 20-plus mountains found throughout the park, including Cadillac Mountain. Throughout these areas of the park, over 330 species of birds have been documented, including warblers, thrushes, eagles, and snowy owls. Some of the 40 species of mammals in this park include deer, foxes, porcupines, snowshoe hares, and bats. In the wetlands ecosystem, which makes up about 20% of the park, visitors can find many of Maine's state-listed rare plants, such as several species of asters, lobelia, and Pickering's reed grass.

The park also includes 14 Great Ponds and 10 smaller ponds; these bodies of water cover just over 7% of the park. Throughout the varying aquatic environments, otters, North American beavers, and 30 species of fish can be found. Along the 40-plus miles of rocky shoreline, a diverse community of intertidal organisms thrive. From the shorelines, visitors may see harbor seals, gray seals, or even harbor porpoises.

— Park Border — Road

American Samoa

American Samoa

Park History

The National Park of American Samoa spans across three islands: Tutuila, Ofu, and Ta'ū. Most of the people living in American Samoa today are Samoans of Polynesian heritage. The Samoan culture is the oldest Polynesian culture, having arrived on the islands from Southwest Asia around 3,000 years ago. This national park exists entirely on land owned by Samoan village councils.

In 1984, Fofó Iosefa Fiti Sunia, the first non-voting delegate to the US House of Representatives from American Samoa, introduced a bill to include American Samoa in the Federal Fish and Wildlife Reservation Act. This would protect the fruit bat, also known as the flying fox, and American Samoa's beautiful rain forest. Spurred on by this initial bill, the National Park of American Samoa was established in 1988. In 1993, the Samoan village councils decided to lease the land for the national park to the National Park Service, allowing the park to be what it is today.

Park Features

As a relatively new national park, there is not much supporting tourist infrastructure surrounding the National Park of American Samoa. However, visitors who love adventure and learning about other cultures will find this to be a can't-miss park.

Uniquely, there is no camping at the park. However, far from being a downside, this gives visitors the wonderful opportunity to participate in the Homestay Program, where visitors can stay in the homes of Samoan families involved in the national park. These families love to welcome their guests into the culture, customs, and daily life of the Samoans. There are also hotels available near the park. Regardless of whether they stay in a home or a hotel, visitors and tourists ought to be conscious and respectful of the Samoan culture; a little research will go a long way in making new friends and avoiding accidental offense.

At the park, there is a wide variety of outdoor exploring that visitors can enjoy. There are many hiking trails, ranging from easy beach walks to challenging rain forest treks. Snorkeling in the beautiful blue waters of the park gives visitors a chance to view the incredibly diverse marine life. There is no way to rent gear, so visitors are advised to bring their own, whether they want to snorkel or scuba dive.

Ecosystem

The National Park of American Samoa consists of three parks on three separate islands, which form a chain of volcanoes that form an arc shape. The national park mainly consists of a tropical rain forest environment. While there are roughly 478 flower plants and ferns that inhabit the islands, the terrestrial species diversity is low. The low diversity could be due to the islands' small size and their remote location.

The only native mammals on the islands are bats, which are extremely important to the area because they pollinate the islands' plants. The most predominant birds seen in this area are the wattled honeyeaters, Samoan starlings, Pacific pigeons, and tropical doves and pigeons. Although the terrestrial biodiversity is low, the marine biodiversity makes up for it with its large numbers of coral and fish species. There are about 250 coral species, which is about one-third of all coral species found throughout the Indo-Pacific region. It is estimated that about 991 fish species live in these areas, the most prominent of which are damselfish, surgeonfish, wrasse, and parrotfish.

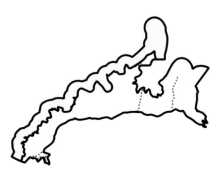

Park Border ··· Trail   Water

Fun Facts:
- Two species of fruit bats can be seen pollinating the island's plants during day and night.
- The youngest island, Ta'u Island, is what remains of a collapsed shield volcano during the Holocene time period. It has sea cliffs that reach heights of over 3,000 feet.

Arches
Utah

Park History

The Fremont and Ancestral Puebloan people inhabited the region of southeastern Utah that now holds Arches National Park until about 700 years ago. Spanish settlers were the first Europeans to explore the area as they searched for routes to California, but they made no attempt to establish a settlement there. The first to settle in the area was a group of Mormons who set up Elk Mountain Mission in 1855. However, conflicts with the locals caused the settlers to abandon the area. Permanent ranches and farms were established in the 1880s and 1890s.

Word of the surrounding area's beauty began to spread, due in part to the local newspaper's regularly published articles describing the rocky wonderland. At the invitation of prospector Alexander Ringhoffer, railroad executive Frank A. Wadleigh visited the area in 1923. Ringhoffer wanted to persuade Wadleigh to build a railroad to the scenic wonders outside the city. Wadleigh was impressed with the landscape and suggested the idea of a national monument to Park Service director Stephen Mather. After government officials examined the area, a proposition to designate the area as a national monument was approved by President Herbert Hoover in 1929.

In 1938, President Franklin D. Roosevelt signed legislation that enlarged the boundaries of the monument as a way to protect the land and sustain tourism. Another enlargement of the area was approved by President Lyndon B. Johnson in 1969. The park was upgraded to national park status in 1971, though the legislation enacted by Congress reduced the boundaries of the park by a considerable margin.

Since its creation, the park has undergone a series of developments, including the addition of trails and areas for rock climbing and camping. Today, over 1.5 million people visit Arches National Park every year to catch stunning views of the 2,000-plus natural sandstone arches.

Park Features

Arches National Park is a wonderland of beautiful red rock and towering geological structures. With over 76,000 acres of land to explore, it can be hard for visitors to choose how to spend their time. The best way to see as much of the park as possible is by car. There are over 40 miles of paved road in Arches, with numerous viewpoints and trailheads along the way. Including ten-minute stops at each viewpoint, the whole trip takes about 4.5 hours.

Hiking, biking, camping, rock climbing, canyoneering, and stargazing are other popular park activities. The only campground at Arches is Devils Garden Campground. The views at Devils Garden are absolutely spectacular, and it is the trailhead for the hike to the 306-foot-long landscape arch. At the height of the busy season, this campground is booked almost every night. Visitors are advised to reserve their stay months in advance.

Ecosystem

Arches National Park contains over 2,000 natural stone arches, along with other red rock formations such as pinnacles, balanced rocks, and fins. Through years of erosion and rock fractures, fins can eventually become arches. Another unique weathering feature is the honeycomb holes, also known as tafoni, that are seen on certain rocks throughout the park.

The park mainly consists of a desert habitat, where some animals have adapted to this harsh environment by being active only at certain times of the day. Some of the nocturnal animals in the park are kangaroo rats, skunks, and owls. Crepuscular animals in the park, or animals most active during dusk and dawn, are mule deer, coyotes, and desert cottontails. Lastly, there are diurnal animals that are most active during the day, such as lizards, snakes, squirrels, and chipmunks. The most common animals in the park are birds, including turkey vultures, ravens, white-throated swifts, or any of the other over 200 species of birds that have been documented at Arches.

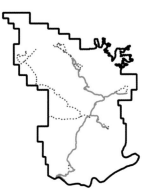

— Park Border — Road ··· Trail

Fun Fact:
- The kangaroo rat is well-adapted to desert life. This hardy rodent doesn't need to drink water to survive because it gets all the moisture it needs from its diet of seeds and plants.

Badlands
South Dakota

Park History

Badlands National Park is so-named because the Lakota people called it *mako sica*, which means "bad lands." They called it this because the clay and jagged canyons are difficult to traverse in rainy weather and hard to survive in during the cold winters and hot summers.

In 1868, the United States signed the Treaty of Fort Laramie with the Oglala, Miniconjou, and Brulé Lakota peoples; the Yanktonai Dakota; and the Arapaho nation. The treaty gave the US authority to punish crime in the area and gave the Sioux ownership of the land in the Great Sioux Reservation. American settlers continued moving into the territory, and the United States seized the land in 1877.

In 1929, Calvin Coolidge authorized Badlands National Monument, which was redesignated as a national park in 1978. In 1980, the US Supreme Court ruled that the violation of the Treaty of Fort Laramie was illegal and that the US government owed the Oglala Lakota Sioux $1 billion. The Sioux refused the money, demanding instead the return of their land in the hopes of creating an entirely tribe-run national park. Over forty years later, this issue of land rights remains unresolved.

Park Features

Badlands National Park has something for everyone. Filled with hiking trails, backcountry routes, campsites, and scenic drives, it's a great spot for visitors of all ages. Families with young children will enjoy participating in the Junior Ranger Program, walking Fossil Exhibit Trail, and visiting the museum exhibits and fossil preparation lab. Those interested in seeing the sights can enjoy scenic views as they drive along Sage Creek Rim Road, Badlands Loop Road, and the perimeter of the South Unit of the Badlands.

With 240,000 acres for visitors to explore, hiking, camping, and photography are some of the most popular activities at Badlands National Park. Hiking trails range from the strenuous Saddle Pass to the long Castle Trail to relaxing boardwalks such as Door Trail. Sunsets and sunrises are stunning in Badlands. Photographers love to capture the soft hues of red, yellow, orange, and brown that bathe the pinnacles and other rock formations with the rising and setting of the sun.

Ecosystem

Badlands National Park is considered a mixed-grass prairie, as the numerous types of grasses lining the park are a variety of heights. The most common grass found in the park is western wheatgrass. Mixed throughout the prairie are sod tables, which sit higher up and consist of broken sections of grass and soil. Many archaeologists have found numerous artifacts within these sod tables, which help shape the story of this region's history.

Throughout the prairie, visitors may catch glimpses of prairie dogs, bison, and pronghorns. Black-footed ferrets are an endangered species, but the park has one of the only self-sustaining populations in the world. Many of these animals help keep the prairie productive by digging holes or rolling in the grass. This activity creates depressions for rainfall to fill and water the vegetation. There are also numerous rock types that can be spotted throughout the park. The layering of these rocks corresponds to different portions of time. Some common rocks in the park are sandstones, siltstones, mudstones, claystones, limestones, volcanic ash, and shale. The park also contains one of the world's richest fossil beds.

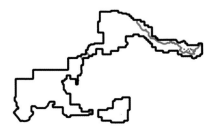

—Park Border — Road ⋯ Trail

Big Bend
Texas

Park History

The Jumano and Chiso Indians, along with other people groups, inhabited Big Bend National Park until the 1700s, when the Mescalero Apaches conquered the region. Later, the Comanches frequently traveled through the area on their way to raid the tribes of the Mexican interior, displacing the Apaches. Spaniards began to explore and occupy the land in the mid-16th century.

Mexico owned this land from 1821 until the treaty of Guadalupe Hidalgo in 1848, in which Mexico gave away over half of its territory to the United States. Throughout the 19th century, what would later become Big Bend National Park was a land of vaqueros, ranchers, pioneers, buffalo soldiers, and Comanche nomads. As it always goes in these stories, the Comanches were eventually forced out of Big Bend by American soldiers paving the way for ranchers and settlers.

By the 1930s, the Americans living in the area all agreed that the land around them should be preserved and protected from overgrazing and industrialization. Texas Canyons State Park was created in 1933 and became Big Bend National Park, as it is today, in 1944.

Park Features

Big Bend National Park is one of the largest, yet one of the least visited, national parks in the United States. It is larger than Yosemite but receives less than half a million visitors per year.

In addition to being a great place to avoid crowds, Big Bend is seen by many as a beautiful land of silence, contrast, and natural wonders. The park consists of miles upon miles of desert, mountain ranges, and scenic drives, making it ideal for a trip of any length.

Big Bend is a wonderful place to hike, backpack, and camp for visitors who seek to bask in the lonely beauty of the natural world. It is also an excellent site for stargazing, as it has the least amount of night pollution out of all the national parks in the contiguous United States. The park's border lies in the middle of the Rio Grande, which means visitors can float or canoe down the river to their hearts' content.

From river tours and stargazing to bird-watching and hiking, Big Bend is the perfect place to go for those who want to explore the wilds of America as they existed hundreds of years ago.

Ecosystem

The Chisos Mountains in Big Bend contain pine-oak-juniper woodlands where the acorn woodpecker, Colima warbler, Scott's oriole, and Mexican jay can be seen. Colima warblers specifically use this park to breed. These mountains are surrounded by the Chihuahuan desert, where numerous cacti and succulents dot the landscape.

The Rio Grande, Tornillo Creek, and Terlingua Creek are three aquatic environments where the Big Bend gambusia, catfish, largemouth bass, and bluegill can be found. In the Rio Grande floodplain, amphibians like the red-spotted toad or Rio Grande leopard frog may be seen, alongside vegetation like cattails, bluebells, dog cholla, and retama trees.

Within the park, there are 75 species of mammals, including the western pipistrelle bat, black bear, rabbits, coyotes, and elk. Big Bend National Park is also an excellent place for bird watching. Along Blue Creek Trail, visitors should keep their eyes and ears open for mourning doves, lucifer hummingbirds, black-throated sparrows, and cactus wren.

━ Park Border ━ Road ⋯ Trail

Biscayne
Florida

Park History

Located south of Miami, Biscayne Bay, the site of Biscayne National Park, was inhabited by Paleo-Indians over 10,000 years ago. After the ice age, this area flooded, leaving the only evidence of the Biscayne Paleo-Indians at the bottom of the sea. Around 2,500 years ago, the people of the Glades culture moved into the area. By the time Europeans arrived in the area in the 16th century, the Tequesta lived in the southeast area of Florida. Due to their ability to live off the sea, the Tequesta were able to devote much of their time to pursuits like religion and art. The arrival of Juan Ponce de León and the Spanish was the beginning of the end of this small tribe, who perished from disease.

It wasn't until the 19th century that Europeans permanently moved into the region. After the American Civil War, Israel Lafayette Jones, one of the few African American landowners in Florida at the time, bought Porgy Key island. By the 1930s, the Jones family was the largest lime producer in East Florida.

In the 1950s, Americans exercised their growing wealth with vacations to Florida. Many wanted to develop the Florida Keys to create hotels, roads, and other tourist amenities. Others wanted to preserve the area for the natural wonder it contained. By 1968, the public support for Biscayne National Monument outweighed the voices of those who wanted to industrialize the area. The Jones family, who still lived in the area, sold their land to the National Park Service. In 1980, Biscayne National Monument was redesignated as Biscayne National Park.

Park Features

Given that it's 95% water, no trip to Biscayne National Park would be complete without some ocean exploring. The most unique feature of Biscayne just might be the Maritime Heritage Trail. As its name implies, this trail is entirely underwater and can be reached only by boat. The trail takes visitors to six different shipwrecks, some as recent as 1966 and others as old as 1878. Some of the sites can be reached by snorkeling, whereas others require scuba gear to reach. The Fowey Rocks Lighthouse, built in 1878 to warn visitors they were approaching a sharp reef, is also part of the Maritime Trail.

Biscayne Bay is also a great place to go boating, fishing, and bird-watching. Visitors can even camp, if they so choose, on Boca Chita Key or Elliot Key. Like everything else in Biscayne National Park, these islands are only reachable by boat.

Ecosystem

Biscayne National Park is a 173,000-acre park that includes the largest marine sanctuary in the US National Park System. Since water encompasses 95% of the park, it comes as no surprise that its four main ecosystems—mangrove forest, bay, subtropical keys, and coral reef—are water-based. Visitors can experience the largest continuous stretch of mangroves left on Florida's east coast. Mangroves are extremely important to marine life and serve as safe shelters and homes for young organisms, including larvae. The branches of these trees allow many birds, such as brown pelicans, to breed and nest.

Other birds seen around the park are loons, herons, white ibises, egrets, sandpipers, cuckoos, and roseate spoonbills. The center of the island has hardwood forests and subtropical vegetation, including the semaphore pricklypear cactus, which is endemic to Florida and limited to the Florida Keys. If visitors are lucky, they may catch a glimpse of the rare and endangered Schaus' swallowtail butterfly. Below the surface and in the warm waters, visitors can experience a wide variety of coral and fish if they choose to dive or snorkel.

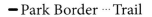

Park Border ··· Trail

Fun Facts:
- About 75% of the bay floor is covered in seagrass.
- The islands that make up the Florida Keys protect the bay from the ocean and act as a barrier to slow down natural disasters such as hurricanes.
- It is estimated that coral reefs cover about half of the park's area.

Black Canyon of the Gunnison
Colorado

Park History

People have been wary of the steep and narrow Black Canyon since mankind first stumbled upon it. The Ute tribe, for whom the state of Utah is named, avoided the canyon due to its rough terrain and the various legends and superstitions surrounding it.

In the first written account of the canyon, penned in 1853, explorer John Williams Gunnison described it as "the roughest, most hilly, and most cut up" land he had ever seen. Like the Ute Indians, he too avoided heading down into the Black Canyon. He was killed by the Utes, who were at war with the Mormons at the time. Black Canyon of the Gunnison National Park was thus named in his honor.

In 1881, the Denver and Rio Grande Railroad was making its way from Denver to Salt Lake City. Originally, engineers hoped to run the railroad straight through the canyon, but when they went down into it, they realized that it would be impossible to build a railroad in such treacherous land.

Park Features

From a distance, the Black Canyon is breathtaking—a deep, dark gash in the surface of the Earth. For centuries, humans have been both afraid of the Black Canyon and drawn to explore its depths. Those willing to brave the dangers of hiking through the designated wilderness of the Black Canyon can make their way from the rim to the bottom, where the Gunnison River flows swiftly. Once in the canyon, expert kayakers can kayak through the Black Canyon, which can be icy cold and fast-flowing. Among rock climbers, the Black Canyon has a reputation for being dangerous and difficult. Only expert climbers who feel confident in their abilities are encouraged to attempt climbing the cliff faces of the canyon.

For those not interested in climbing steep cliffs or paddling through rapid flowing rivers, there are scenic drives and rim trail hikes that also provide incredible views and a sense of adventure. From the rim of the canyon, visitors can both see and feel how severely the Black Canyon cuts into the surrounding green landscape.

Ecosystem

The most stunning geological feature of the Black Canyon of the Gunnison National Park is, of course, the Black Canyon. The Black Canyon was carved by the Gunnison River, whose fast and powerful flow eroded away the gneiss and schist formed during the Precambrian period. At its steepest point, it drops 240 feet per mile, and at its narrowest point, it is only 40 feet wide. The steepness and narrowness of the aptly named Black Canyon causes some parts of the canyon to be shrouded in darkness for over 23 hours a day.

There are four main life zones within the park, including pinyon/juniper forest, oak flats, inner canyon, and the Gunnison river. The Black Canyon is home to many bird species that aren't daunted by its dizzying heights and sudden cliffs. The great horned owl, mountain bluebird, peregrine falcon, and canyon wren are just a few of the species you might spot on a trip to this national park. Visitors may see river otters or rainbow and brown trout swimming in the river. The park is also home to over 46 mammal species, including mule deer, cottontail rabbits, and black bears.

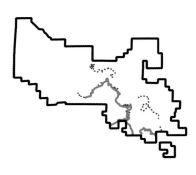

— Park Border — Road ··· Trail

Bryce Canyon
Utah

Park History

Originally named Utah National Park upon entrance into the Park Service in 1924, Bryce Canyon enjoyed little notoriety amongst early Mormon settlers throughout the 19th century. The canyon did not provide much in the way of grazing or farmland, so pioneers had little use for the place. It was not until the early 1900's that the area began to draw visitors. This long period of inactivity can also be attributed to the lack of real roads, rails, or waterways around the area, making tourism more difficult than places like Yosemite or the Rocky Mountains.

In 1915, Forest Service supervisor J. W. Humphrey discovered Bryce Canyon for himself and could not be "dragged away" from its beauty. As tourism to the West increased, so did Bryce Canyon's popularity. Even the Great Depression would not reduce visitation to the park, and from 1929 to 1939, numbers increased fivefold. Following the end of World War II and the construction of a highway from Zion to Bryce, visitation rose to over a quarter of a million people annually, even though the park was only open for spring, summer, and fall. Today, nearly three million people travel to Bryce Canyon every year to enjoy it for themselves.

Park Features

At just 56 square miles, Bryce Canyon is on the smaller side of the national parks in the US, meaning that very determined visitors can see nearly the entire area in a day. Roads and lookout points across Bryce make the most iconic locations incredibly accessible. The most popular of these is Thor's Hammer at Sunset Point, which is a 100-yard walk from a nearby parking lot. Sunset Point also happens to be the best location for sunrise photography. From Sunset Point, visitors can walk down into the midst of the hoodoos (tall, thin spires of rock), regardless of age or ability, as the paths are smooth and only moderately inclined. It's not uncommon to see courageous parents pushing strollers into the beautiful red- and orange-hued valley.

Ecosystem

Bryce Canyon spans over 2,000 feet of elevation, from Yovimpa Point to the bottom of Fairyland Loop Trail, providing the park with several distinct climate zones. The distinct sedimentation and colorful hoodoos are the most obvious aspects of the park. Some visitors don't realize that far below the rim, little meadows of wildflowers and forests are home to hundreds of animal species.

Bryce Canyon hosts a Christmas Bird Count to help assess bird populations for osprey, nutcrackers, swallows, condors, falcons, and more. The park is also home to 59 species of mammals, ranging from foxes and cougars to antelope and prairie dogs. Since the park is cooler, there are not too many species of reptiles, but visitors should look out for the Great Basin rattlesnake on warm summer days. Besides the venomous snake, the park is home to horned lizards, salamanders, and other safe but exciting creatures worth observing. In 2019, the park gained International Dark Sky status and is a great place for visitors to stargaze.

— Park Border — Road ⋯ Trail

Canyonlands
Utah

Park History

The area of Canyonlands National Park was inhabited by the Fremont and Puebloan people roughly 2,000 years ago. They mainly focused on agriculture and lived in local villages year-round to tend to their crops. By AD 1200, the populations were becoming crowded, so large swathes of people moved to the far reaches of the area, now known as the Needles. Around AD 1300, the living conditions became too unstable, causing the Puebloans to migrate south.

European explorers first entered the Canyonlands in the 1800s, with John N. Macomb and later John Wesley Powell exploring the area by river. Powell's expeditions in 1869 and 1871 provided the first details of the area's geology and topography. It was around this time that cattle were frequently herded through the area, often using the Canyonlands to graze.

Beginning in the 1950s, the area was explored and mined for uranium, but not enough ore was found for it to be profitable. Arches National Monument superintendent Bates Wilson explored the area and began advocating for the establishment of a national park. Determined to make it happen, he provided a series of tours for government officials so they could see the marvels of the Canyonlands. One of these tours was joined by Secretary of the Interior Stewart Udall, who took the idea to the capitol. On September 12, 1964, President Lyndon B. Johnson signed the bill establishing Canyonlands National Park.

Park Features

Canyonlands National Park is divided into four unique districts, the most popular of which is the Island in the Sky, which attracts over 75% of the park's visitors. Located in the northern region of the park, the enormous mesa resting on 1,000-foot sandstone cliffs can be viewed from many different overlooks along the scenic road that follows the rim. Each overlook provides a slightly different viewpoint across the many miles of red rock canyons. The Island in the Sky district of the park is known for being the easiest to visit, especially if visitors are short on time. For the more explorative tourists, there are numerous other roads and backcountry hiking trails available.

Ecosystem

Canyonlands National Park has a variety of ecosystems, from riparian zones and ephemeral pools to desert. The desert within the park forms the heart of the Colorado Plateau and is considered a cold desert, where temperatures can fluctuate over 40 degrees in just 24 hours. It also receives more rain than many deserts, with an average of about 9 inches annually. This rain helps fill natural sandstone basins known as ephemeral pools or potholes. Visitors should look for tall spires of multicolored rock formations formed from deposits of sand blown from the west along with deposits from mountains.

The Colorado River flows through the park and helps create a nice riparian zone for a variety of shrubs and trees, such as Fremont cottonwood, willow, water birch, and boxelder. Beavers live in riverbank dens because these waterways are too large for them to build dams. Other animals that might be seen along the riparian zones are muskrats, river otters, raccoons, and skunks. Because of the many insects living around aquatic habitats, riparian zones are a great place to bird-watch. Some common birds seen within the park are great blue herons, Canada geese, canyon wrens, and yellow-breasted chats.

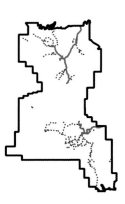

—Park Border — Road ⋯ Trail

Capitol Reef
Utah

Park History

Located in south-central Utah, the land known today as Capitol Reef National Park has been home to people for thousands of years. The earliest known people groups in the area were the Paleo-Indians. Years later, the Fremont people, hunter-gatherers who practiced supplemental farming, moved into the area. They lived in Utah for about a thousand years before disappearing and being replaced by the Paiute, Ute, and other tribes.

In 1853, John C. Fremont, on a mission to find a railroad route to the Pacific, made his way through the rock monoliths of Capitol Reef. Many naturalists, geologists, and geographers traveled through the area between 1869 and 1872, forming theories about the unique topography of the region.

The first American settlers in the area were the Mormons, who set out across Utah to establish towns and proselytize the Native Americans. They established the towns of Fremont, Bicknell, Torrey, and Junction (now called Fruita). Twelve-year-old Nettie Behunin was the first school teacher in Fruita, and her one-room schoolhouse still stands today.

In 1937, after years of local residents promoting the region and lobbying for its protection, Franklin D. Roosevelt designated 37,711 acres of land as Capitol Reef National Monument. In 1971, Capitol Reef National Monument was upgraded to national park status by Richard Nixon.

Park Features

The unique geological features of Capitol Reef may be the park's most striking aspect. Visitors can explore the land however they would like, whether it be through a scenic drive, a hiking trail, or a backcountry trek. Cathedral Valley is an incredible stop for geology enthusiasts or anyone who enjoys unique sights. The Bentonite Hills, smooth domes striped in various soft shades of purple, red, and gray, are also incredible to see whether by foot or car. The Waterpocket Fold is also an incredible sight up close, as visitors can see the dramatic angle at which the land has bent and curved from erosion.

Before hiking or driving through Capitol Reef, visitors should check the weather conditions and visit the National Park Service website to make sure they are adequately prepared for the trip. For those who want to experience Capitol Reef after dark, there are many options available. The park has one developed campground, two primitive campgrounds, and backcountry options to fit a variety of visitor needs.

Ecosystem

Capitol Reef National Park is named after its rock formations: white domes of sandstone that resemble capitol buildings and steep rocky cliffs that resemble reefs. Due to many years of erosion, visitors can see a beautiful cross-section of the 19 different layers of rock, all of which vary in color. While visiting the park, visitors can also view rocky canyons, cliffs, domes, and bridges. Another interesting geological feature is the black boulders, ancient volcanic rocks that have been eroded and polished by glacial floods.

The park is part of a "high" desert, which receives more rain and is cooler than a typical desert. Despite the extra rain, springs, tinajas, and potholes are still vital water sources for fauna living in the park. While some of these water sources are only temporary, the Fremont River flows through the park and is considered a year-round water source along with Sulphur Creek. These aquatic habitats support some fish, like several species of suckers, speckled dace, and mottled sculpin. The park has also documented over 230 bird species and 58 mammal species, including chipmunks, deer, and ringtails.

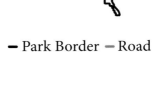

— Park Border — Road

Fun Fact:
- Another popular rock feature can be found in Cathedral Valley. These unique formations, called "cathedrals," are free-standing monoliths of sandstone that resemble temples or cathedrals.

Carlsbad Caverns
New Mexico

Park History

In 1898, a young cowboy named Jim White was going about his normal routine of rounding up cattle when he noticed smoke billowing in the distance. In fear of a wildfire, White rode toward the smoke to investigate, only to realize as he got closer that he was not riding toward smoke. Pouring out of a nearby cave was an enormous group of Brazilian free-tailed bats. White would eventually venture into the cave, exploring the different chambers, or "rooms," and naming them as he went.

Several years later, White encountered a photographer named Ray V. Davis. Jim shared stories of his findings and invited Ray to take pictures of the different rooms. Davis would take an extensive photographic record of the caverns over the next 3-4 years. These pictures attracted local interest and soon the attention of the rest of the nation. During the 1920s, visitors came from all across the country to see the spacious chambers.

In 1923, after much advocacy by Jim White, the cave and surrounding areas were established as the Carlsbad Cave National Monument. Its growing popularity and visitation prompted national park status, which was eventually granted in 1930.

As the park gained traction, it also received complaints that the 750-foot ramp was too long of a walk when making the trip back up to the surface. In 1932, two elevators were constructed to take visitors in and out of the caverns with ease.

Park Features

Accessible by hike or via elevator, this national park's biggest attraction is its namesake: the Carlsbad Cavern. This enormous cave was home to Native American tribes over 1,000 years ago but was abandoned, leaving nothing behind but mysterious drawings and carvings on the walls. It was rediscovered in 1898 by 16-year-old cowboy Jim White, who explored the caves over the next several years and gave names to the various "rooms."

Balloon Ballroom is a room located above the main entrance to the cave. When it was first discovered, it was accessed by floating a collection of helium balloons to the passageway. Bat Cave is a large passage that contains the majority of the cave's bat population. The Big Room is the most spacious of all the chambers in the cave, measuring over 350,000 square feet.

There are over 20 named rooms, with more chambers and mesmerizing features being discovered over time. In October of 2019, a specialized expedition discovered a pristine cave pool that is connected to a body of water known as the "Lake of Liquid Sky." The pool is thought to have remained untouched by humans and contains several unique colonies of bacteria.

Ecosystem

Carlsbad Caverns National Park is known for its numerous caves, such as Carlsbad Cavern and the 140-mile-long Lechuguilla Cave. For geology enthusiasts, Lechuguilla Cave has large and rare speleothems, or cave formations. These caves are home to large colonies of cave swallows and Brazilian free-tailed bats. There are also numerous crustaceans living among the caves.

The park also includes part of the Chihuahuan Desert, which is the most biologically diverse desert in the Western Hemisphere. Within the park, there are about 26 species or subspecies of cacti, which create a great food source for numerous animals. The cacti also serve as an area for certain birds to build nests, like the cactus wren. More than 50% of the park consists of shrubland environments including montane and desert shrubland. There have been 67 mammal species documented in the park, including javelina, ringtails, and mule deer. While a lot of the park is considered more dry, there is a permanent water source and riparian area known as Rattlesnake Springs. Here, two native fish species, the roundnose minnow and greenthroat darter, can be found.

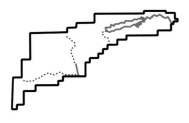

— Park Border — Road ··· Trail

Fun Facts:
- Carlsbad Cavern was created from hydrogen-sulfide-rich waters that mixed with rainwater to form sulfuric acid. This acid dissolved the limestone to create the Carlsbad Cavern, where visitors can see large sums of gypsum deposits, clay, and silt.
- Out of the 67 different mammal species found within the park, 17 are bat species.

Channel Islands
California

Park History

The Chumash people inhabited the Channel Islands for thousands of years before they moved to mainland California. Those who lived on the islands traveled using tomols, canoes made from redwood logs.

Spanish explorer Juan Rodríguez Cabrillo arrived at the Channel Islands in 1542. From then on, resource exploitation and foreign disease gradually pushed the Chumash off the islands. By the early 19th century, all the Chumash had moved to the mainland. The islands were used for ranching until the early 20th century, at which point they became largely used by the US military. Two of the islands, Anacapa and Santa Barbara, were designated as a national monument in 1938. By 1980, Santa Cruz, San Miguel, and Santa Rosa were also under National Park Service management, and all five islands were established as Channel Islands National Park.

Park Features

Each of the islands in Channel Islands National Park offers something different to visitors. None of the islands have services, so visitors must come prepared. Anacapa Island is great for a day trip to go hiking, camping, or wildlife viewing. For those who come well-prepared, Anacapa is a good place to enjoy solitude. Santa Cruz Island is the easiest of the Channel Islands to get to, has water and equipment rentals, and enjoys great weather. Scorpion Beach on Santa Cruz is a beautiful place to kayak, dive, snorkel, and swim in the crystal clear waters. Santa Barbara is a cliff island, which makes for interesting views and challenging hikes. It is a great place for water sports. Intertidal animals can sometimes be spotted here at low tide.

San Miguel Island can be quite difficult to get to, as high winds are common around this area, and visitors must have a permit to travel there. Once on the island, visitors are not allowed to hike off the trail due to the island's history as a former bombing range. The hiking trails are spectacular, and majestic seabirds and stealthy island foxes can be spotted by those on the lookout for them. Santa Rosa Island can also be difficult to get to due to high wind speeds. Water sports are limited at this island due to the wind, but hiking is spectacular. Visitors can hike along flat beaches or up to the rugged Black Mountain.

Ecosystem

Channel Islands National Park includes five of the eight Channel Islands off the Southern California coast—each providing unique and diverse environments. The park includes a variety of communities and habitats, including floodplains, wetlands, rocky intertidal zones, grassland, kelp forests, and seagrass beds. Marine life such as seals, sea lions, dolphins, numerous fish, barnacles, sea stars, and crustaceans live around the islands and deep submarine canyons.

Due to these islands being isolated from the mainland, the biological diversity is rather low. However, there are species evolving into separate subspecies on each island to adapt to the varying climates and conditions. For example, the fox and deer mouse, which are two of the only four native mammals found on the islands, have evolved into eight unique mammal species. It is easier for birds to reach the islands, allowing visitors to see hummingbirds, bald eagles, sparrows, finches, and peregrine falcons. There are close to 800 plant taxa inhabiting the islands, with about half of those being lichen species (organisms that are a unique combination of algae and fungi).

➡Park Border

Fun Facts:
- The Channel Islands are an essential nesting and feeding ground for 99% of seabirds in Southern California and contain the only breeding colonies of California brown pelicans in the state.
- It is estimated that the islands provide about one-third of the state's total lichen species.

Congaree
South Carolina

Park History

People have used, explored, and shaped the floodplain of what is now Congaree National Park for over 13,000 years. In return, the floodplains have played a part in shaping the lives of thousands of people. The Congaree Indians used the land to hunt and fish. Hernando de Soto, a Spanish conquistador, found the area mysterious and intriguing, though not nearly as filled with gold and riches as he might have hoped. American revolutionaries set up ambushes for the British among the massive trees of this hardwood forest. For escaped African American slaves, the floodplains were a place of refuge and freedom, and after emancipation, many were baptized in its waters.

By the late 19th century, the Santee River Cypress Logging Company began to extract resources from the area at an alarming rate. In the 1970s, the Congaree Swamp National Protection Association united with the Sierra Club to convince South Carolina senators to establish Congaree Swamp as a national monument. Congress redesignated and renamed Congaree Swamp as Congaree National Park in 2003, preserving the vast and varied cultural history of the Congaree floodplains.

Park Features

Congaree National Park is most known for its beautiful bottomland hardwood forest, the tallest deciduous forest in the US. The trees are the primary attraction of the park, and people come from miles around to hike through them. There are almost 2.5 miles of boardwalk and over 25 miles of hiking trails available to explore these beautiful and unique forests.

In addition to hiking through the trees, visitors can get to know the Congaree River by kayaking or canoeing down the 15-mile Cedar Creek Canoe Trail. Otters, turtles, wading birds, and even alligators can sometimes be seen along the canoe trail. Congaree also offers camping, backcountry camping, and fishing.

SPEED
LIMIT
25

Fun Facts:
- The Ptarmigan bird species have feathered feet that help them combat the snow, and they also have adapted to dive or burrow into snow for insulation against the cold.
- Wood frogs live in puddles and ponds in the summer and freeze solid in the winter. They survive the freezing process by pumping glucose throughout their bodies to keep ice crystals from forming inside their cells, even though the rest of them is frozen solid.

Gateway Arch

Missouri

Park History

There is an abundance of history surrounding the Gateway Arch National Park in St. Louis. It is known as the "Gateway to the West" and was constructed from 1963 to 1965. The arch represents many crucial moments in the history of the US. It commemorates the city of St. Louis' role in westward expansion, and it is just a short walk from the location of the infamous Dred Scott trial.

Dred Scott v. Sandford took place in St. Louis' Old Courthouse. Dred Scott and his wife Harriet were both born to enslavement. When Scott was 50 years old, in 1846, he decided it was time to sue for his freedom. He had lived in free territories in the United States and had legal grounds for the suit. After eleven long years of trial, the Supreme Court decided that Dred and Harriet Scott had no legal grounds to sue, that the Missouri Compromise was unconstitutional, and that no African American had the right to be a citizen of the United States.

The Court's decision was devastating for the Scotts and for every African American and their allies. The Dred Scott v. Sandford ruling is recognized as directly contributing to tensions between the North and South, increasing injustice for African Americans, and realizing the dawn of the Civil War.

Park Features

The main attraction of Gateway Arch is, of course, the Arch itself. The Arch is 630 feet tall and 630 feet wide at its base, weighing 886 tons. It is an astounding feat of engineering. The architect, Eero Saarinen, designed a massive structure that viewers would immediately recognize as the Gateway to the West. It was then up to the engineers, such as Fred Severud, to figure out how to make that design into reality.

The Arch would be too tall for any normal crane, so they used climbing cranes, which could be drawn up the legs of the Arch as they were being built. The formulas used to calculate the curve and dimensions of the Arch took hours upon hours, as their construction team didn't have access to the computer power that exists today. Installing the final four-foot segment of steel required over 500 tons of pressure to push the top of the legs far enough apart to insert it into place.

Visitors can ride up the Arch in a tram to see an incredible panoramic view of St. Louis. In addition to riding to the top of the Arch, visitors can learn about the city of St. Louis in a museum underneath and stop at a gift shop to pick up souvenirs and educational material. The Old Courthouse, the site of the Dred Scott case, is just a 10-minute walk from the Arch.

Ecosystem

The land around Gateway Arch is largely developed, as it exists primarily around a man-made monument. When visiting the Arch, one can walk along the Mississippi River and the surrounding park. The Upper Mississippi flows from Lake Itasca in Minnesota to St. Louis and gives a home to over 125 species of fish and 30 species of mussels.

While the Mississippi River is far cleaner than it was in decades past, the river still suffers from pollutants and runoff from nearby agriculture and industry. The Mississippi is the main ecological system that can be seen near the Arch.

However, as it is right in the middle of St. Louis, this national park is within walking distance from many other man-made attractions. Historical buildings, museums, and restaurants can all be found within a short distance from the park.

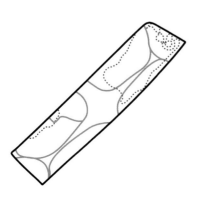

━ Park Border ━ Road ┄ Trail

Glacier
Montana

Park History

Human habitation of the Glacier National Park area dates back thousands of years. Before Western explorers arrived, the Blackfeet, Salish, and Kootenai tribes hunted and lived in the region. The fur trade brought the first European settlers in the early 1800s, and the European population grew slowly until the advent of the railroad. Prospectors, hunters, and miners arrived with the trains, and tourists were close behind. By 1892, one could find rental cabins, restaurants, pack horses, and guided trips into the glaciers.

In 1910, the area was established as the 9th national park. Chalets and lodges were constructed to accommodate the increase in tourism. Nearly two decades of work led to the completion of the "Going-to-the-Sun Road," which connected the western and eastern regions of the park. Construction on visitor centers at Logan Pass and St. Mary ended in 1966 and 1967, respectively. At the same time, glaciers began to recede on a consistent basis. Over the past five decades, ten named glaciers have completely melted. Research projects have begun to monitor and study the trend as well as the rocks, bones, and other remains left by the melting ice.

Park Features

Logan Pass is easily one of the most popular features of Glacier National Park. Going-to-the-Sun Road takes visitors to the pass from either the western or eastern regions of the park. The road winds through forests, along lakes, and up cliff faces. It is nearly a 30-minute drive from either side of the park, but the vistas along the way make the drive worth taking. From Logan Pass, which reaches a height of 6,646 feet, guests can see for miles along the deep valleys. In summer months, wildflowers pepper the views with color, and wildlife is close at hand, despite the heavy foot traffic. Hikers will often arrive early to park and hike down the mountain to one of the bus stops for a return trip. Sunset at Logan Pass is simply spectacular and a must for artists, photographers, and sight-seers.

Lake McDonald makes for another excellent stop. Just past the western Glacier Park entrance, Lake McDonald is easy to get to and attracts millions of visitors every year. At ten miles long and 500 feet deep, it is the largest lake in the park. Surrounded by mountains and ancient forests, it is perfect for a picnic, a quick dip, or camping. Boat rentals are available, as is a shuttle service that stops along the lakeside and camping areas. For visitors looking for a short day hike, several excellent options exist along the edges of Lake McDonald, but they will be warned to look out for bears.

Ecosystem

Glacier's ecosystem is as diverse as it is delicate. Thousands of plant and animal species thrive in the park. A favorite park of bird watchers, Glacier is a perfect place to see bald and golden eagles as well as the harlequin duck. The park is also known for its bear population, as it is one of the last areas in the lower 48 states where grizzlies are still common. Also common to Glacier are mountain goats, bighorn sheep, elk, and more.

Geologically, Glacier is a very special place, due to the namesake glaciers across the park. In order to be classified as a glacier, the ice in question must be at least 25 acres in size and move slowly due to the force of gravity and its significant weight. The weight of a glacier compresses the bottom layer of snow into ice, reducing friction and allowing the entire sheet to slowly slip along the sides of mountains. This scraping action creates iconic U-shaped valleys, moraines, and cirques (scoop-like impressions carved into the mountainsides).

Additionally, the cliff faces are often a variety of shades of red and green. This is due to iron in the stone being oxidized (green) or not oxidized (red).

— Park Border — Road ⋯ Trail

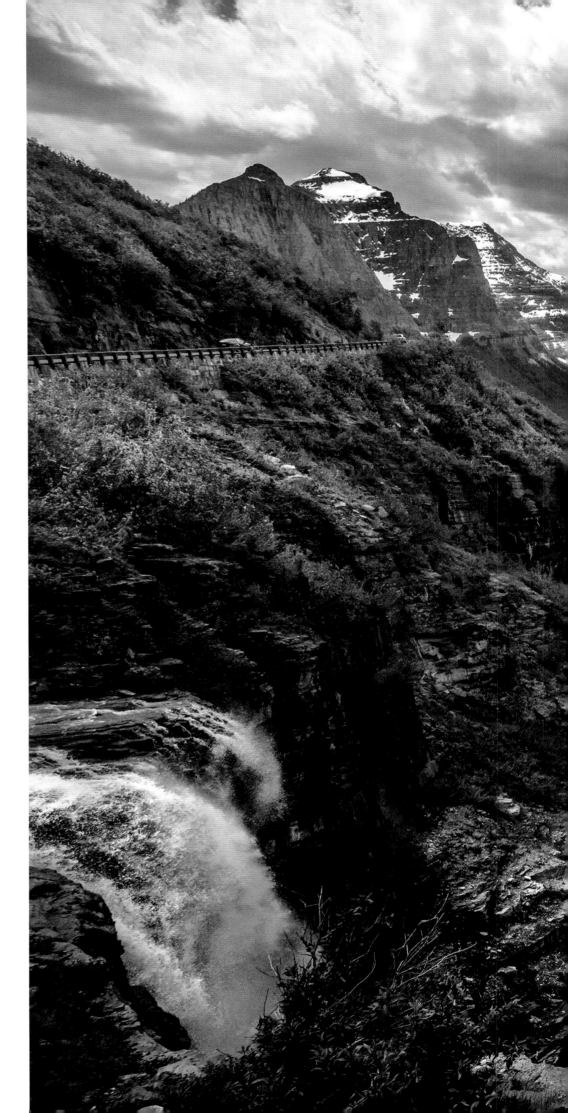

Crater Lake
Oregon

Park History

Following an eruption of epic proportions, the majority of Mount Mazama in Oregon collapsed and formed an enormous caldera, a cauldron-like volcanic crater, which holds what is now known as Crater Lake. The first pioneers to discover the lake were gold miners who were searching for a mine called "Lost Cabin" in 1853. They discovered the lake on their journey and proclaimed that it contained the bluest water they had ever seen. Their quest for gold was ultimately unsuccessful, and the discovery of the lake was soon forgotten.

Several other explorers rediscovered the lake multiple times over the next 40 years, and Sergeant Orsen Stearns became the first non-Native American to reach the shore of Crater Lake in 1865. National park status for the area surrounding the lake was promoted by journalist William G. Steel, who helped map the lake in 1886. The conservation movement was on an upswing in the US, which helped achieve Steel's efforts to create the local Cascade Range Forest Reserve in 1893. On May 22, 1902, Crater Lake National Park was established by President Theodore Roosevelt.

Steel continued to work and lobby for further improvement and expansion of the park and saw the opening of the Crater Lake Lodge in 1915. Built on the rim of the lake, with magnificent views of the surrounding peaks, the 71-room hotel drew many visitors when it first opened. A few years later in 1918, the scenic Rim Drive was developed, allowing visitors to explore a 33-mile loop around the lake. Soon, highways leading to the park were built to encourage further tourism. Today, over 750,000 people visit the park every year to see the stunning views of the lake and explore the mountain trails that surround the enormous crater.

Park Features

Crater Lake National Park contains several mountainous features that were created by the eruption of Mount Mazama, including the Pumice Desert, the Pinnacles, and Timber Crater. However, the most awe-inspiring feature of the park is the sparkling blue water the area was named after: Crater Lake.

The lake sits inside an enormous caldera that was formed by the collapse of Mount Mazama. As multiple explorers discovered and rediscovered the lake during the 1800s, the name changed from Blue Lake to Lake Majesty to Crater Lake. The lake is the deepest in the US at 1,949 feet, and it stretches 5 by 6 miles across.

The Klamath tribe of Native Americans who originally inhabited the area and witnessed the eruption, regard the lake and surrounding area as a sacred, spiritual site. It was long believed by the tribe that the lake was so sacred that any person who gazed upon the lake would die, and many would not acknowledge the lake's existence when asked about it by white explorers.

The lake contains two small islands: Wizard Island and Phantom Ship. These were created by lava eruptions that occurred after the initial eruption of Mount Mazama. Because of the lack of inlets and tributaries, there is an absence of pollutants, which makes the water that fills the lake some of the purest in the world. Scientists in 1997 recorded a record clarity of 142 feet; for comparison, an average reading is around 33 feet.

Ecosystem

Crater Lake National Park has more than 40 caves; 31 of these caves exist within the rim of the caldera, and many others are near the lake surface. No fish existed in the park until the lake was stocked with kokanee salmon and rainbow trout. A 30-foot mountain hemlock log, commonly known as The Old Man, has its upper three feet exposed above the lake's water.

While Crater Lake is most known for rock formations and the giant lake after which it was named, the park also consists of 180,000 acres of streams, wet meadows, forests, and pumice fields. Pumice fields are large barren areas where volcanic rock deposits of pumice and scoria remain. Due to the rocks' high porosity and the poor soil composition found here, plants grow very slowly, or not at all, in this environment. Some common mammals that visitors may see are golden-mantled ground squirrels, black bears, deer, and bats. In the winter, American martens and snowshoe hares are known to inhabit the areas. Eagles and peregrine falcons often nest around the cliffs of the caldera, while Canada jays, hummingbirds, and spotted owls may be seen flying through the park.

—Park Border — Road ⸳⸳⸳ Trail

Cuyahoga Valley
Ohio

Park History

The Lenape nation were the original residents of the Cuyahoga Valley and are considered to be the ancestors of many other Native nations in the area. The Lenape were steadily and forcefully pushed from their land by numerous violent conflicts and broken treaties with the US. Today, the Lenape are scattered throughout the US and are often referred to as the Delaware Nation.

The US gradually claimed Ohio starting in 1805, when they purchased 500,000 acres from the various Native nations that lived there, including the Lenape. By 1870, American urbanites frequently came to Cuyahoga Valley for leisurely boat rides and other relaxing outdoor activities.

In 1929, the estate of Hayward Kendall, a businessman from Cleveland, donated 430 acres to the state of Ohio, requesting that the property be used as a park. In the 1930s, the Civilian Conservation Corps worked to further maintain the area. By the 1960s, local citizens feared that urban growth from Cleveland and Akron would soon take over the wilderness of Cuyahoga Valley. They petitioned the state and national government to protect the area, and in response, President Gerald Ford established Cuyahoga Valley as a National Recreation Area in 1974.

In 2000, the area was redesignated as a national park, making Cuyahoga Valley the only national park in Ohio and the only national park to have first been a National Recreation Area.

Park Features

Cuyahoga Valley National Park is popular with visitors who enjoy fishing, kayaking, backpacking, and hiking. The most iconic hiking route in Cuyahoga is along the 20-mile section of the Towpath Trail contained within the park. This trail follows the path of what used to be the Ohio and Erie Canal, which was built between 1825 and 1832 to connect the wilderness of Ohio with the eastern United States. The path that comprises Towpath Trail today was the very same path that mules trotted along to tow boats down the Erie Canal almost 200 years ago.

In addition to hiking the Towpath Trail, Cuyahoga Valley offers rewarding outdoor adventures to visitors in every season. From skiing, sledding, snowshoeing, and ice fishing, to camping, biking, and even horseback riding, visitors to the valley can venture through the wilds of Ohio at any time of year by whatever method they choose.

Ecosystem

Cuyahoga Valley resides in the Great Lakes Basin. It has a humid continental climate, with temperatures ranging from around 20-35°F during the winter and 60-80°F during the summer months. This climate is perfect for the variety of animals that live in the park, such as raccoons, muskrats, coyotes, skunks, red foxes, beavers, deer, geese, and bats.

The Cuyahoga River, which runs through the park, is itself a fascinating natural feature. The river is 100 miles long, and almost 200 individual streams feed into it. The course of the river is unique, flowing first southwest and then north toward Lake Erie in a "V" shape. In the industrial era, much of the river was polluted heavily, to the point that it was completely devoid of life. Today, the health of the Cuyahoga River is back on track as ecologists and other scientists monitor its water and surrounding habitats.

Fish, frogs, amphibians, and insects such as the pickerel frog, Jefferson's salamander, emerald shiner, and viceroy butterfly all call the ecosystem of Cuyahoga their home.

— Park Border — Road ⋯ Trail

Death Valley
California/Nevada

Park History

The Timbisha, also known as the Shoshone or the Panamint, have lived in Death Valley for over a thousand years. They were primarily nomadic, living in the valley during the cooler winter months and spending the scorching summers in the nearby mountains.

A group of pioneers seeking to prospect in California became lost in the Mojave desert in 1849. Suffering dehydration and starvation, they traveled through the desert for months, even losing one member to the harsh elements. The rest had to eat their oxen to survive but eventually hiked out of the valley on foot, where they were rescued by Mexican cowboys. As they left the valley, the story goes, one woman said, "Goodbye, Death Valley," giving the area the name we know it by today.

The American population in Death Valley boomed once borax was discovered. Gold, silver, lead, and copper were also discovered, though not in the great quantities pioneers and prospectors hoped for.

The darkest moment in the history of Death Valley occurred in 1942, when Japanese Americans were placed in concentration camps there after the US went to war against Japan. Today, many people make frequent pilgrimages to Manzanar, the site of one of the concentration camps, to pay their respects to the innocents who suffered there.

Manzanar and other sites were protected forever when Death Valley was declared a biosphere reserve by UNESCO in 1984 and designated as a national park in 1994.

Park Features

As the hottest, driest, and lowest national park, Death Valley attracts over 1.5 million visitors each year. It's a beautiful place to be overwhelmed by the simultaneous beauty and harshness of nature. At every national park, one must take common sense precautions in order to have a safe and fun experience. That is especially true at Death Valley. The National Park Service warns visitors to drink plenty of water and electrolytes and to be on the lookout for signs of heat stroke and dehydration. During the summer, high temperatures ranging from 110-134°F can cause vehicles to break down from overheated engines. There is little to no cell phone coverage in Death Valley, so officials recommend that drivers and their passengers stay close to their vehicles in the event that they break down.

With the proper precautions and research, Death Valley is a great place to visit. It is thrilling to explore at any time of day or night. The Borax Works, Mesquite Sand Flat Dunes, and Badwater Basin are some of the top places for visitors of all experience levels to sight-see, hike, and stargaze.

Ecosystem

As the hottest place on earth, Death Valley boasts fascinating ecology. Routinely reaching temperatures of 110-120°F, Death Valley's climate makes it difficult, though not impossible, for many creatures to survive. For example, wildflowers are able to bloom in the spring, watered by snowmelt and winter rains. Surprisingly, Death Valley contains over 600 springs and ponds and even has a waterfall. The national park rests in a depression of land surrounded by mountain ranges, called a graben. The surrounding mountains help to funnel warm air back into the valley, keeping it hotter for longer.

The lowest portion of the valley, Badwater Basin, is 282 feet below sea level, making it the lowest point in North America. The basin is frequently victim to flash flooding and gets its name from the salt coating the basin floor, making any water present undrinkable. Despite its harsh name, the Badwater Basin is home to living creatures. Perhaps one of the smallest and most resilient residents is the Death Valley pupfish. Despite reaching an average length of only 1.5 inches, the pupfish is tough enough to live in water that has four times the salinity of the ocean.

—Park Border — Road ··· Trail

Denali
Alaska

Park Features

The main attraction of the six-million-acre Denali National Park and Preserve is the mountain itself. Glaciers make up 16% of the park, with five large glaciers flowing from the slopes of Denali, some more than 30 miles long.

Due to the extreme weather and low barometric pressure, scaling Denali is an extremely challenging feat. Temperatures can reach -75°F, with wind chills reaching -118°F. Over 75% of the mountain is permanently covered with snow and ice. The first successful climbing expedition to the summit of Denali was in 1913. More than 32,000 climbers have endeavored to reach the summit, but only a few have managed to reach the top.

There are a variety of ways to explore the breathtaking scenery of Denali and the area around it, but the way to really see the mountain up close is to book a flightseeing tour via helicopter or small aircraft. Some flightseeing tours even land on a glacier. Viewing Denali National Park from the sky is a unique and unforgettable experience.

Park History

Standing at 20,310 feet, Denali, North America's tallest mountain, is part of the 600-mile-long Alaska Range situated between the Alaska Peninsula and the Alaska-Canada border. Throughout history, this massive mountain has been called by many different names. The name Denali was given by an Alaskan Native tribe and translates to "the Great One" in the Athabaskan language. Russian explorer Andrei Glazunov gave it the name Tenada, which means "Great Mountain." Bolshaya Gora, which means "Big One," is another Russian name used for the mountain.

In 1867, the United States purchased Alaska from Russia. In 1889, gold prospector Frank Densmore's enthusiasm for the great mountain resulted in many other prospectors in the area calling it Densmore Mountain. In 1896, the mountain was unofficially named Mount McKinley by gold prospector William Dickey. That name was made official by the federal government of the United States in 1917 to commemorate President William McKinley, who was assassinated in 1901. In 1975, the state of Alaska requested that the mountain be officially recognized as Denali, the common name used in the state, but the efforts were blocked. In 2015, the mountain's name was officially changed from Mount McKinley to Denali.

Efforts by conservationists Charles Sheldon and Belmore Browne led to the establishment of Mount McKinley National Park in 1917. In 1980, Mt. McKinley National Park, Denali National Monument, and Denali Preserve were incorporated to establish Denali National Park and Preserve. The park has over six million acres and is the third-largest park in the United States behind two other Alaska parks, Gates of the Arctic National Park and Wrangell-St. Elias National Park and Preserve, which is the largest. Over 400,000 visitors travel to Denali each year to enjoy the untamed wilderness of frozen tundra, glacial lakes, towering mountains, forests, and incredible wildlife.

Ecosystem

Denali National Park includes low-elevation taiga forests, high alpine tundra environments, and snowy mountains. Within the six million acres of land in the park there is only one road in and out. The park contains the tallest mountain in North America, which reaches a height of 20,310 feet.

Trees such as black and white spruce and paper birch tend to grow best in the lowland area, causing forests to appear more full. The subalpine region has more shrub vegetation and fewer trees. The highest plant diversity in the park exists at the highest elevation, although this area reaches the upper growth limit for plants. Similar to the subalpine region, dwarf birch, willows, black crowberry, and bog blueberry exist at such heights.

Common wildlife in the park are moose, caribou, Dall sheep, wolves, and grizzly bears. Red foxes and arctic ground squirrels inhabit the more snowy regions. There are over 160 species of birds, including Canada jays, golden eagles, ptarmigans, and gyrfalcons. Due to the cold temperatures, there are no reptiles found in the park.

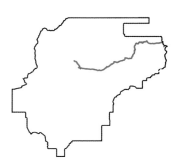

— Park Border — Road

Fun Facts:
- This was the first national park created to protect wildlife.
- Although temperatures in this park get far below freezing, there is one amphibian, the wood frog, that lives in the park. To survive these temperatures, this frog uses special chemicals to protect its cells from damage by freezing solid in the winter.

Dry Tortugas
Florida

Park History

Dry Tortugas may seem to be a strange name for a national park that is surrounded entirely by water. The park's name goes back to the 16th century, when Juan Ponce de León, the first European to see the islands, caught over 150 sea turtles in the surrounding area. The lack of fresh water to be found on the island makes it "dry" in terms of drinking water, hence the name Dry Tortugas.

Today, the Dry Tortugas are known not only for their turtles and beautiful reefs but also for the abundance of military history that remains near the island. When the US purchased Florida from Spain in the early 19th century, the American government saw it as a key militaristic stronghold in the Gulf of Mexico. Work began on Fort Jefferson in 1846 but was left unfinished due to the start of the American Civil War. After the Civil War, the fort was used as a military prison, most famously holding Dr. Samuel Mudd and three other men who were imprisoned for conspiring to assassinate Abraham Lincoln. Mudd famously inscribed a quote from Dante's *Inferno* on the walls of his cell: "Whoso entereth here leaveth all hope behind." Mudd was freed after helping the prison survive an outbreak of yellow fever.

Park Features

From snorkeling and diving to fishing and boating, there is a host of things to do at Dry Tortugas National Park. The island itself is surrounded by a moat, and visitors are encouraged to swim around the outside of the moat wall to view the myriad of historical artifacts and marine life that make their home in the surrounding waters.

The most famous dive in Dry Tortugas is the wreck of a three-masted sailing ship named Avanti that wrecked on Loggerhead Reef in 1901, known today as the Windjammer.

The Windjammer site is a favorite of both experienced scuba divers and casual snorkelers, as the wreck spans a range of depths from zero feet, where part of the ship peaks above the surface of the water, to 20 feet, where the ship rests among the marine life. An incredible diversity of ocean life, from giant jellyfish to colorful coral, can be seen in various parts of the wreck.

Glacier Bay
Alaska

Park History

When European explorers arrived in Glacier Bay in 1786, the Tlingit people were the dominant people group in the area. The ancestors of the Tlingit may have even lived in the bay itself, before the glacier advanced upon the valley that would become the bay. In 1786, Jean François de Galaup, comte de Lapérouse became the first European to enter the land that would become Glacier Bay National Park. Russian explorers and fur traders also made their way over and were the dominant European presence in the area until the 1880s, when Americans arrived in search of gold.

John Muir, the famous American writer and naturalist, visited the area in 1879. He wrote about it in his book *Travels in Alaska*, and Muir Glacier was named in his honor. William Skinner Cooper, an American ecologist from Minnesota, made his own trip to Glacier Bay in 1922, inspired by John Muir's writings. Cooper was so inspired and amazed by the beauty and natural value of the land that he petitioned Glacier Bay be protected from development and industrialization. In 1925, Glacier Bay National Monument was established under the Coolidge administration. The passing of the Alaska National Interest Lands Conservation Act made more of Alaskan land eligible for protection. In 1980, Glacier Bay National Monument and surrounding lands were designated as Glacier Bay National Park and Preserve.

Park Features

Comprising over 3.3 million acres and situated on the southern coast of Alaska, Glacier Bay offers a diverse selection of activities for visitors. Much of the area is wilderness, making it a wonderfully remote place for backpacking, camping, and even mountaineering.

Bartlett Cove, which used to be completely glaciated, is the only developed area in the park. Here, visitors can take guided tours, walk along the shore, and explore various hiking trails. The Huna Tribal House, a gathering place for the Tlingit to take part in ceremonies, meetings, and other events, is in this area of the park. Visitors can stop by the house to admire the art and participate in various cultural programs run by the Tlingit. Kayaking is also popular in this area.

Given that Glacier Bay is on the coast, boating is popular all over the park. Cruises, tour boats, charter boats, and private vessels are frequently seen exploring and enjoying the beautiful landscapes of Glacier Bay.

Ecosystem

Animals residing within Glacier Bay National Park are usually located 30 miles or less from the coast, allowing them easy access to food. Visitors may see hungry bears, river otters, or coyotes walking along the shoreline in search of prey or carcasses that may have washed ashore.

The marine environment makes up about one-fifth of the park and creates several ecosystems, such as the intertidal and subtidal zones, with over 200 species of fish documented within the park. From the coast, visitors may observe sea otters, seals, or even humpback whales swimming in the ocean. Crows or ravens can be seen snatching clams and mussels up and dropping them from high elevations to open their shells.

The park contains 7 tidewater glaciers, which are glaciers that flow all the way down to the sea. As the saltwater crashes against the glaciers, icebergs are formed, creating a nice place to rest for gulls, bald eagles, or even seals. Further inland consists of a temperate rain forest of evergreens, western hemlocks, lichens, mosses, and blueberries. Mountain goats, moose, and porcupines are often found roaming in these areas.

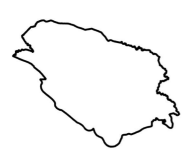

━ Park Border

Grand Canyon
Arizona

Park History

The Grand Canyon's human history predates recorded times. When European settlers and explorers finally arrived in the mid-1500s, Native Americans had been calling this place home for thousands of years. As far as historians know, this area was home to several tribes, including the Hopi, Apache, Navajo, and more. Many of these names will sound familiar to park visitors, as several features and trails have been named in their honor.

For centuries, most Westerners assumed the Canyon was unnavigable. In the 1800s, that all changed as the federal government commissioned several expeditions. John Wesley Powell was the most notable leader of the Grand Canyon's exploration, spending many months in the area researching and mapping the Colorado River. Decades later, prospector Dan Hogan purchased some 20 acres for what would become the Orphan Mine. The mine produced copper for years, and eventually the property also became a trading post and tourist attraction.

In 1951, it was discovered that the area was rich with uranium. The old copper mine was refurbished with heavy equipment to manage dozens of tons of rock and ore each day. When demand for uranium plummeted in the 1960s, the area passed into federal ownership and protection. Visitors can still see the Orphan Mine site in the cliff face of the Canyon. Other mines and tourist attractions also closed through the 20th century due to legal battles over ownership rights or low demand. Today, the National Park Service is responsible for the maintenance and conservation of the entire Grand Canyon area.

Park Features

There is an endless list of things to do and places to see at Grand Canyon National Park. The South Rim is the more commercially developed of the two rims and therefore has more resources for those who want to do a lot of exploring without a lot of hiking. The bus schedule is very consistent and travels dozens of miles along the rim, providing easy access to the beautiful views. At the main village on the South Rim, visitors have access to hiking trailheads, historic buildings, lodging, restaurants, exhibits, and a visitor center. The Bright Angel Trailhead begins there and takes day hikers below the rim, six miles toward the bottom of the canyon.

About 25 miles east of the village is the Desert View Tower. Designed by renowned architect Mary Colter and built during the Great Depression, the style of the structure follows that of native tribal design. Towering 70 feet into the air, the views from the top are spectacular. Even farther east, one can find the iconic Horseshoe Bend, as the Colorado River curves back around upon itself. Until recently, this site had no infrastructure, so overcrowding meant dangerous situations along the edge of the cliffs, which drop hundreds of feet to the river below.

On the North Rim, there are far fewer crowds, lending to a quieter experience. The North Rim Visitor Center is only open during summer months, and during that time, the schedule is full of opportunities to attend ranger-led programs, meet Native American Tribes during heritage events, hike along trails, bird watch, and more. The North Rim stands several hundred feet above the South Rim, making the vistas even more dramatic and beautiful.

Ecosystem

Geology is likely one of the first things that leaps to visitors' minds when thinking about the Grand Canyon, and rightfully so, as it is one of the most studied geologic locations in the world. But there is more to this semi-arid landscape than the rock formations that photographers love. With over 1,500 plant species, 350 bird species, and nearly 100 mammal species, there is no lack of exciting wildlife to look out for.

Visitors may spot pronghorns, bison, bighorn sheep, elk, mule deer, foxes, and more. But quite often, it is what you cannot see that makes a place extra special, and that is true for the Grand Canyon. Creatures like the rarely seen ringtail, javelina, and mountain lion—along with dozens of other species—all play a part in the delicate ecosystem balance at the Grand Canyon.

Since the area is mostly desert and arid in its ecological makeup, most would not think about the native fish and water-dependent species that have called the canyon home over the centuries. Since the construction of two massive dams (Hoover at the west end, Glen Canyon at the east end) the indigenous water life has been severely impacted.

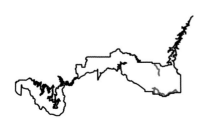

— Park Border — Road

Grand Teton
Wyoming

Park History

Long before Western Europeans discovered the Grand Teton Mountain Range, Native Americans called this place their home for thousands of years. The area, rich in edible plants and herds of buffalo, proved perfect for tribes like the Shoshone, Blackfoot, Crow, Flathead, Nez Perce and more. In the early 1800s, the Lewis and Clark expedition passed by the area, and a man named John Colter left their expedition to explore the Teton region. After him, other trappers and hunters followed in his footsteps, setting up outposts through the mid-19th century.

Homesteaders and ranchers soon followed, settling in nearby Jackson Hole. Tourism exploded in the early 1900s. Visitors would come and stay at a "dude ranch" to experience the edge of civilization while still having access to the comforts of a bed and home-cooked meals. When John D. Rockefeller Jr. discovered the massive commercialization taking place around Jackson Hole, he purchased tens of thousands of acres to create a conservation society. Shortly afterward, in 1929, Grand Teton National Park was established.

Park Features

In wintertime, thousands visit the Tetons for some of the best skiing in America. But for those who want to experience nature at its most warm and lively, summertime at Grand Teton is ideal. The Aerial Tram takes guests to the Teton Crest, traveling over 2,700 feet in just over 10 minutes. At the top, restaurants, incredible panoramic views, and activities such as hiking and yoga are available to all.

For visitors seeking water activities, Jenny Lake is a must. The crystal clear snowmelt water makes for excellent kayaking and canoeing. Sunrise is ideal for birding and photography everywhere in the park, but especially around the lakes. Be aware, however, as it is not too uncommon to see a black bear foraging for berries along less-busy paths.

Those looking to camp or hike in Grand Teton National Park could not pick a more beautiful place to do so. Typically, for overnight trips into the mountains, there is a reservation and lottery system to obtain campsites. The Teton Crest Trail is one of the more popular hikes among avid backpackers. After riding the tram up the mountain face, hikers travel 30 to 50 miles along the peaks of the Tetons. The views are breathtaking, as is the altitude. At over 10,000 feet, it is not uncommon to experience some altitude sickness.

Ecosystem

Sitting on a fault line, the Grand Tetons are composed of granite and a high-grade metamorphic rock called gneiss. Sedimentary rocks can also be seen in cliff faces of the mountains, often filled with fossils. In addition to this geological history, glaciers have scooped large sections of the mountainsides away, leaving beautiful, smooth valleys.

The ecosystem, though delicate, is vibrant and diverse. With elk, moose, bear, bighorn sheep, and over 300 bird species calling the park home, there is no lack of sights to see in the Grand Tetons. There is also a variety of ecosystems that support life in the park, including floodplains, forests, wetlands, ponds, and lakes.

To see it all, guests should try to walk around Leigh Lake during the early morning hours. Birds, fish, and moose are active far before humans start their recreation. All of the lakes are open for visitors to swim and undertake in non-motorized boating activities. Hiking into the mountains is another way for visitors to guarantee a glimpse at wildlife.

— Park Border — Road ⋯ Trail

Great Basin
Nevada

Park History

Great Basin National Park is named for the Great Basin region, which includes almost all of Nevada and some of Oregon, Utah, California, Idaho, Wyoming, and Mexico. Great Basin National Park covers 77,180 acres of land in Nevada.

Human inhabitance at Great Basin began with the Paleo-Indians. After the Paleo-Indians and the Great Basin Archaic people left the region, the Fremont moved in, around 1,500 years ago. Not much is known about the Fremont. They lived in adobe villages, farmed and hunted, and traded with other villages. Around 500-700 years ago, the Fremont vanished from the archaeological record. No one is sure whether they were displaced or assimilated by other groups or if they became nomadic due to climate changes. The Shoshone moved to the Great Basin region about 700 years ago and still live in that area today.

In the early 1800s, American trappers made their way to Nevada. Mines and ranches were established throughout the mid and late 1800s. Ranching was an important part of the culture of the Great Basin. One rancher, Absalom Lehman, forever left his mark on the Great Basin when he discovered and named the Lehman caves in 1885. The unique geology of the caves led to the creation of Lehman National Monument in 1922 and contributed to the establishment of Great Basin National Park in 1986.

Park Features

Great Basin offers everything from hiking through the vast desert, to skiing down snow-covered mountains, to plunging into the depths of wild caves. Great Basin averages only a little over 90,000 visitors each year, making it a national park where one can truly experience the feeling of being alone in nature. There are also plenty of guided tours for those without the experience or desire to go it alone. The Lehman Caves are popular with all visitors, and there are seven wild caves available for those with wild cave permits. There are about 60 miles of official hiking trails in addition to backcountry areas. Visitors can also horseback ride and bring pack animals such as mules, burros, and llamas.

Visitors can still enjoy backcountry camping in the winter and have the opportunity to see the park in both the height of summer and the midst of winter. Skiing and snowshoeing are also popular winter activities. Winter is the slowest season at Great Basin, so those seeking a quiet and icily beautiful outdoor experience will not want to miss an opportunity to visit.

Ecosystem

Great Basin National Park contains caves, deserts, and glacial environments. The park includes the Great Basin Desert, which is considered a "cold desert," as most of the precipitation received comes from snow. This cooler desert is possible due to the numerous mountain ranges in the park. While the park is located in the desert, there are also six subalpine lakes, along with 10 permanent streams.

Some common mammals living in the desert and sagebrush are kangaroo rats and black-tailed jack rabbits. At higher elevations, there are six subalpine lakes, but all are fairly small and support numerous species of phytoplankton and insects. At these heights, visitors can see the only glacier in Nevada, Wheeler Peak Glacier, near the base of Wheeler Peak.

Within the park, there are over 41,000 acres of karst, which supports 40 known caves. The most popular cave, Lehman Cave, is the longest cave in Nevada at over 2 miles long. Interestingly, park staff found a new freshwater shrimp in one of their caves, Model Cave.

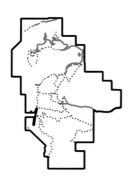

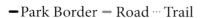
━Park Border ━ Road ⋯ Trail

Great Sand Dunes
Colorado

Park History

The first to live in San Luis Valley, where Great Sand Dunes National Park and Preserve resides, was the Ute tribe. The Navajo and Apaches were also familiar with the region. One people group, from the Tewa pueblos by the Rio Grande, recognize one of the lakes near the dunes as the birthing place of their people, believing that their ancestors emerged from the waters into the world.

The first European to set foot in San Luis Valley was Don Diego de Vargas in the 17th century. Many famous explorers such as John C. Fremont, Zebulon Pike, and John Gunnison traveled through the valley at one point or another. Eventually, settlers made their homes in the valley, setting up ranches, homesteads, and mines.

By the 1920s, the Americans who lived in the San Luis Valley had grown quite fond of the Great Sand Dunes area. In an effort to protect the dunes against increasing mining and industrialization, the Philanthropic Educational Organization (PEO) Sisterhood championed the effort to secure a national monument designation for the Great Sand Dunes. In the late 1990s, the monument was redesignated as a national park.

Park Features

Great Sand Dunes National Park and Preserve is home to the tallest sand dunes in North America. Just standing amidst the dunes gazing up at their peaks is an experience worth having.

However, besides just admiring the landscape, there are some exciting things to do at the Great Sand Dunes, one of which is sandboarding and sand sledding. Those wishing to shred the sand dunes must rent equipment from outside the park and be sure to read up on the safety precautions. It is about 0.7 miles from the parking area to the first small slopes, which are perfect for families with young children. The first large dune is 1.25 miles away from the parking area.

Medano Creek is another popular attraction for adults and kids alike. Depending on the time of year, visitors can surf, swim, skimboard, float, and splash around in the refreshing water.

Ecosystem

Great Sand Dunes National Park contains the tallest dunes in North America within its dunefield, but surprisingly, this consists of only 10% of the sand deposit. The majority of the park's sand deposit is found in a sand sheet, or a sandy grassland region. In this area, elk and pronghorn are common. Mice, kangaroo rats, and short-horned lizards may also be scurrying and crawling through these areas. Visitors can see a lot of different types of dunes in this park, including star dunes, transverse dunes, parabolic dunes, barchan dunes, and reversing dunes, which are the most common.

While the park is known for its sand dunes, there are also wetlands, conifer and aspen forests, alpine lakes, and tundra environments. Within the wetlands, sandhill cranes, amphibians, and freshwater shrimp can be found, while the forests are home to mountain lions, mule deer, and northern pygmy owls. Trout and some amphibians inhabit the cooler alpine lakes. Ptarmigans, marmots, bighorn sheep, and brown-capped rosy finches have been documented in the alpine tundra.

Park Border Road Trail

Great Smoky Mountains
Tennessee/North Carolina

Park History

The region that now contains Great Smoky Mountains National Park was part of the Cherokees' homeland before European settlers arrived in the 18th century. The majority of the native population was relocated by President Andrew Jackson's Indian Removal Act.

As European settlers moved in, logging became a wildly successful industry, which resulted in the destruction of the area's natural beauty. In an effort to preserve the land, locals and visitors came together and started to raise funds. The National Park Service had the desire to establish a park in the eastern part of the country, but there was still not enough money to make it happen, nor was there enough federally owned land on which to build one. In the end, it took donations from John D. Rockefeller and private citizens from Tennessee and North Carolina to allow the park to be built piece by piece. The area was slowly developed over the next 8 years and was established as Great Smoky Mountains National Park on June 15, 1934. This was the first park to be funded in part by federal funds.

The unforgettable landscapes, along with attractions such as Dollywood and Ripley's Aquarium of the Smokies, swiftly made the park the most visited national park in the United States, with over 11 million tourists visiting the park every year. The volume of tourism to the park contributes over $2 billion to the local economy every year.

Park Features

The most popular attraction of Great Smoky Mountains National Park is an isolated valley called Cades Cove. Located in the Tennessee section of the park, this broad valley is surrounded by scenic mountain views and an abundant display of wildlife, providing its 2 million annual visitors the most stunning views of the park.

The cove is named after a leader of the Tsiya'hi Indian tribe known as Chief Kade, though very little else is known about him. The Cherokee claims to the area were eradicated after the Treaty of Calhoun in 1819, and the tribes were relocated to Oklahoma. Throughout the 19th century, European settlers developed the area, building houses, farms, and businesses. This boom in development suffered after the Civil War and did not fully recover until the early 1900s.

As the formation of Great Smoky Mountains National Park began, inhabitants of Cades Cove pushed back, not wanting their land and livelihood to be disrupted. Though initially promised that the valley would not be included in the new park, a bill was passed in 1927 that allowed the Park Commission to seize the property within the valley. After a large dispute, it was officially finalized by the Secretary of the Interior that the valley was indeed necessary for the park.

Visitors can view Cades Cove via the Cades Cove Loop Road, an 11-mile one-way loop that circles the cove. Along the route are several buildings that are representative of 19th-century pioneer life in the area as maintained by the National Park Service.

Ecosystem

With a large range in elevation (850-6,643 feet), Great Smoky Mountains National Park is the most biodiverse park in the National Park System. Almost 95% of the park is forested and consists of five major forest types, including cove hardwood forests, spruce-fir forests, northern hardwood, hemlock, and pine-and-oak forests.

Throughout all areas of the forest, visitors may spot one of the 200 species of birds documented in the park. While the infamous American black bear is probably the most well-known animal living within the park, the park is known as the "Salamander Capital of the World" because it is home to roughly 30 species of salamanders. If visitors plan their trip accordingly, they could view the synchronous fireflies that light up the park approximately 2-3 weeks each year during their mating season.

There are about 2,100 miles of streams, with about 67 native fish species inhabiting these areas, including brook trout, spotfin chub, and duskytail darters. Brook trout are the only trout species native to the park and compete with the non-native rainbow trout for food and habitat.

— Park Border — Road ··· Trail

Fun Facts:
- The cove hardwood forest is the most botanically diverse region in the park, with 40-60 different tree or shrub species.
- While the wetlands consist of less than 1% of the park, about 25% of species documented in the park are linked to this environment.

Guadalupe Mountains
Texas

Park History

Many different groups have inhabited the Guadalupe Mountains area, leaving behind scattered remnants of baskets, pottery, and art. The Spanish did not attempt to establish any large-scale settlements, but they did introduce horses to the area in the 1500s. This had a lasting impact on the Apache tribes that roamed the land, as the horses aided their largely nomadic lifestyle.

The first extensive assessment of the area was taken in the 1850s by surveyors who were heading up railroads nearby. As more temporary settlements were founded, there arose conflicts with the Apache, who were raiding settlers' homes. Lieutenant H. B. Cushing led a band of troops to the area and effectively wiped out two of the Apache camps, driving the tribes into reservations.

The Rader brothers, early settlers in the Guadalupe Mountains, built the first permanent building in the area, now known as Frijole Ranch, in 1876. During the 1920s and 1930s, more ranches were built, which led to further development of the surrounding land.

The idea to preserve the land as a national park was proposed in 1923, but it was not seriously considered until much later when Wallace Pratt became involved. Pratt was a geologist and early explorer of McKittrick Canyon. He started buying land and building houses in the canyon. In an effort to further the preservation of the area, Wallace donated roughly 6,000 acres in McKittrick Canyon. The government soon purchased 80,000 additional acres, and the bill to establish the park passed Congress in 1966. Construction of upgraded park facilities began in 1977, while resource management focused on identifying and preserving the natural resources found in the park. By 1988, the park's development was essentially complete. Visitation to the park by this time had risen to about 178,000 people annually, and the park has maintained an average of about 200,000 annual visitors since then.

Park Features

In the heart of Guadalupe Mountains National Park stands the highest natural point in the state of Texas and one of the park's most popular attractions: Guadalupe Peak. Also known as Signal Peak, the 8,751-foot mountain is part of the Guadalupe Mountain range that stretches from southeastern New Mexico to West Texas.

Visitors can take a strenuous 8.5-mile round-trip hike to see fantastic views of the park and its various ecosystems. The summit is marked by a stainless steel pyramid commemorating the 100th anniversary of the Butterfield Overland Mail, a stagecoach that used to pass just south of the mountain.

Ecosystem

Guadalupe Mountains National Park is known for the 8,000-foot peak, El Capitan. This limestone cliff was formed from an accumulation of fossilized invertebrate skeletons from different areas of reef. The channels and canyons in the park are made of sandstone and siltstone beds. On and around these rocky canyons, visitors may see ringtails, rock squirrels, snakes, and tree lizards. The park also includes part of the Chihuahuan Desert, where prickly pear cacti, ocotillos, agaves, honey mesquite, and yuccas can be found. Many of the animals that live here exhibit a nocturnal lifestyle to beat the heat of the warm days.

While this park is known for its fossilized reef formation and desert environment, mountains and riparian ecosystems can also be found. Elk, black bears, and porcupines live in ponderosa pine and Douglas fir forests along the mountains. Oaks and maples line the sides of streams. Mule deer are probably the most common animals that visitors see in the riparian ecosystem, as well as skunks and raccoons.

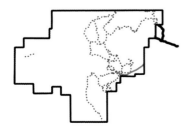

━Park Border ━ Road ⋯ Trail

Fun Fact:
- Couch's spadefoot toad has made some incredible adaptations to the dry environment in Guadalupe Mountains National Park. It lives underground to survive dry spells, can slow its metabolism, and can lose up to 50% of its water.

Haleakalā
Hawaii

Park History

The island of Maui has been inhabited by Polynesian and Hawaiian people for hundreds of years. Each generation of people was known to hold the great Haleakalā volcano as a sacred place, restricting the surrounding area for ceremonial purposes.

The first written record of non-Hawaiians reaching the summit was made in 1828 by a group of three missionaries. At the summit, they found a large multi-colored crater that had been formed by erosion. In 1841, Charles Mills explored the crater and mapped it, using traditional Hawaiian names for many landmarks and structures.

Lorrin A. Thurston, grandson of missionary and explorer Asa Thurston, strongly advocated for a national park to be established in the area to preserve the land. He used The Honolulu Adviser, a newspaper he owned, to distribute editorials discussing the idea of a new park. After much debate and several failed attempts, legislation to create a national park passed, and Hawaii National Park was established by President Woodrow Wilson on August 1, 1916.

After further development, the park was split into two parks in 1961: Haleakalā National Park and Hawai'i Volcanoes National Park. In 1969, the boundaries were expanded to include the coastal area of 'Ohe'o. Today, Haleakalā National Park's 30,000 acres are visited by over 1 million people every year.

Park Features

The namesake and centerpiece of Haleakalā National Park is the great Haleakalā volcano. Haleakalā, or "the house of the sun," stands at 10,023 feet and forms more than 75% of the island of Maui. It is classified as a dormant volcano, with the last eruption estimated to have been in 1790 and the next eruption possibly occurring in the next 100 years.

The early Hawaiian people believed that the grandmother of the demigod Maui lived at the summit of Haleakalā. Legend has it that his grandmother helped him capture the sun and slow its pace through the sky for his mother, Hina, so her handmade cloths would have enough time to dry in the sun.

Visitors can take one of two main trails into the mountain: Sliding Sands Trail or Halemau'u Trail. The walking trails at the summit are known for their challenging uphill climb and thin air, but there is never a shortage of tourists using the trails to get a glimpse of the sunrise as it hits the mountain.

Ecosystem

Haleakalā National Park is located on one of the Hawaiian islands, making it one of the most geographically isolated landmasses in the world. Two main features of the park are the Haleakalā Volcano and the Haleakalā Crater, the latter of which resembles a valley that was formed from erosion. Along the summit region, an alpine desert zone exists that is quite barren due to the porous ground. However, visitors should keep their eyes open for two species of silversword that can be found withstanding the harsh environment. The silversword is a rare, delicate plant with thin, silver-green leaves that can live to be up to 90 years old. Both the Haleakalā silversword and the delicate silversword are endemic, meaning that they can only be found in this area.

At lower elevations in the park, the environment consists of subalpine shrubland, where more vegetation can be found, including several native shrubs and trees like the 'ōhi'a lehua tree that displays rich red blossoms or the kūkaenēnē, whose dark purple-black berries are a favorite fruit of the endangered and endemic Hawaiian goose. There are areas of the park that get 120-400 inches of rain annually, creating a rain forest ecosystem.

— Park Border — Road ··· Trail

Fun Facts:
- Within the Haleakalā Crater, 14 cinder cones can be seen. These were formed from gas being trapped in lava after an eruption
- The largest known nesting colony of Hawaiian petrels has been documented at the top of Mount Haleakalā.

Hawai'i Volcanoes

Hawaii

Park History

Thirty miles south of Hilo, in the southern region of Hawaii's largest island, lies one of the world's most active volcanoes, Kīlauea. Traditionally, the volcano was considered the sacred home of Pele, the Hawaiian volcano goddess, who the natives would visit to offer gifts. In 1823, the first non-native visitors discovered the site. Missionary William Ellis kept journals of his explorations and noted that he "stopped and trembled" upon seeing the erupting volcano.

Word of the spectacle soon spread, and the volcano became a tourist destination. In fact, enough people started to visit on a regular basis that local businessmen started to run a series of hotels located at the rim of the volcano. An original hotel from 1877, known as "Volcano House" still stands onsite and houses the Volcano Art Center.

Politician Lorrin A. Thurston, grandson of one of the original Western discoverers of the site, held an interest in preserving the area as a national park. He enjoyed exploring the area and was determined to preserve it, so he published several editorials in favor of establishing the land as a national park in The Honolulu Advertiser newspaper, which he owned at the time. The site gained popularity, and when volcanologist Thomas Jagger founded the Hawaiian Volcano Observatory in 1912, Thurston's lobbying efforts became successful. Four years later, President Woodrow Wilson signed legislation to establish Hawaii National Park. It became the first national park to be established in a United States territory.

In 1961, the park was renamed Hawai'i Volcanoes National Park after it was split from Haleakalā National Park. Today, over 2 million people visit the park annually.

Park Features

At the heart of Hawai'i Volcanoes National Park is Kīlauea, the youngest volcano on the island of Hawaii and the largest active volcano in the world. In the late 1700s, an unusually violent eruption trapped a group of warriors in the area, as well as women and children who were nearby. A record of footprints from this time was found in the cooled, hardened lava and is still visible today.

Kīlauea has erupted 34 times since 1952, keeping it high on the list of the world's most active volcanoes. As the eruptive episodes of the volcano come and go, visitation to the site is closely monitored. In March of 2008, a small explosion launched debris over an area of 74 acres, though no sight of lava was reported. From 2008 to 2018, an active lava pond could be seen at the summit, which eventually drained following an eruption.

Visitors can explore the summit of the 4,090-foot volcano by taking a trip down Crater Rim Drive. This scenic route will take you through a surprisingly diverse selection of desert and tropical rain forest while providing a majestic view of the rumbling Kīlauea volcano.

Ecosystem

Hawai'i Volcanoes National Park contains two of the world's most active volcanoes: Kīlauea and Mauna Loa. The active volcanoes and volcanic eruptions have created unique features throughout the park, such as cinder cones, Pele's hair, steam vents, sulphur banks, and lava trees. Ka'ū Desert, although not a true desert due to the amount of rainfall it receives, is barren and does not produce much vegetation due to sulfur dioxide from nearby volcano vents mixing with rain to produce acid rain.

Besides the volcanoes, the park is full of tropical rain forests. About 90% of its native terrestrial flora and fauna are considered unique to the area. The state bird of Hawaii, the Hawaiian goose, inhabits areas within the park and feeds on numerous berries that shrubs and trees produce. Other plants produce nectar, which is an important food source for many birds in the park, including native birds like the honeycreepers. In the water and beaches surrounding the park, visitors can see hawksbills and green sea turtles.

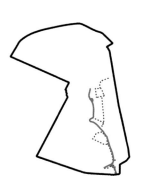

━Park Border ━ Road ⋯ Trail

Fun Facts:

- The park is home to the Kazumura lava tube system, a 40-mile-long underground passageway formed by lava. This system is thought to be the longest lava tube cave in the world.
- There are about 200 species of ferns found throughout the park, including Hāpu'u, which is the largest tree fern in the state and can reach heights up to 35 feet.
- Pele's hair, which can be seen on the ground near the summit of Kilauea, is a form of lava that is described as long, thin strands of volcanic glass formed from gas during a volcanic eruption.

Hot Springs
Arkansas

Park History

The history of Hot Springs, Arkansas, is a mixture of both good and bad. Established as a federal reservation in 1832, the city had already become known for its healing waters, earning it the nickname "America's Spa." Unfortunately, the springs weren't always such a relaxing place to be. During the American Civil War, tensions increased as Confederate and Union soldiers passed through the city of Hot Springs in turn. After the war, racial segregation continued in the bath houses. African Americans were only allowed to use certain facilities after operating hours, which remained true until Hot Springs became a National Park in 1921. Decades later, W. T. Bailey, a black architect, designed the Pythian Bathhouse and Sanitarium. Shortly after, Dr. Timothy L. Bottoms, a black Army veteran, practiced podiatry and foot surgery at the Fordyce Bathhouse. Over the years, dozens of Bathhouses have operated along "Bathhouse Row." However, only two remain in operation today, as all the others have been repurposed as conference centers, museums, and other types of venues.

Park Features

Although the bathhouses are certainly the attraction prospective visitors tend to think of first, equally popular with visitors is the Hot Springs Mountain Tower. Rising over 200 feet into the sky above the nearby Hot Springs Mountain, the observation tower allows visitors to climb or ride to views that stretch far beyond the bathhouses in the valley below. For the more adventurous guests, there is a 1.5-mile trail from downtown Hot Springs up to the parking lot around the tower.

Ecosystem

Hot Springs is known for the mineral springs that run below the park, and for good reason. The folds and fault lines in the crust allow the water to be heated to almost 200°F, before it emerges from the sandstone rocks at about 150°F. This hot water has dissolved a number of minerals found in the rock through which it has traveled, including calcium, magnesium, potassium, and more. There are 47 springs still flowing and active in the park.

As for the ecology at Hot Springs National Park, the area is thriving with amphibians, reptiles, birds, and mammals. While many people believe organisms cannot inhabit the warm waters found in the springs, thermophiles such as blue-green algae, thermophilic bacteria, ostracods, and nanonobacteria thrive in these environments within the park. Hot Springs is home to nearly several species of salamanders, frogs, and toads.

Every Christmas, the local residents of Hot Springs participate in a bird-watching inventory, recording nearly a hundred different species in the area around the park. Some common birds documented in the park are herons, warblers, and sparrows.

━ Park Border ━ Road ⋯ Trail

Indiana Dunes

Indiana

Park History

Indiana Dunes National Park has long been a lonely, quiet place. There were no permanent inhabitants of the region until people of the Hopewell culture moved in and lived in the region from about 200 BC to AD 800. After that, there were no permanent inhabitants until the 1800s, when Native American villages began to pop up throughout the Indiana Dunes. These native villages were quickly pushed out by American settlers, who began to industrialize the region.

In 1899, botanist Henry Cowles, today recognized as "the father of plant ecology" in the US, published an article on the incredible flora in the Indiana Dunes. This article and Cowles' passion for the Indiana Dunes started a movement to preserve the area.

However, at the same time Cowles and others were making an attempt to preserve the dunes, industry in the region was booming. Steel mills, power plants, and glass makers rushed to the dunes to capitalize on their resources. The largest sand dune, standing at 200 feet high, was carted off bit by bit to make glass fruit jars.

The "Save the Dunes" movement made good progress until the US entered World War I and subsequently fell into the Great Depression. As the country began to recover, the Save the Dunes council was able to purchase the Cowles Bog, the first protected piece of land in what would later become the Indiana Dunes National Park. In 1966, Congress passed a bill to create the Indiana Dunes National Lakeshore, protecting over 8,000 acres of land and water. On February 15th, 2019, Congress redesignated Indiana Dunes National Lakeshore, which had grown to over 15,000 acres, as Indiana Dunes National Park.

Park Features

Indiana Dunes has a wide variety of features to suit all kinds of guests. There are over 15 miles of beaches in the park. Visitors can swim in Lake Michigan during the summer and hike the dunes. The hiking trails provide beautiful views and adventures no matter the season. In the summer, the lush green trees and glittering blue water of Lake Michigan lend to a warm, vibrant experience. In the winter, the trees and land are covered in a blanket of snow, and visitors can enjoy the peaceful solitude of the quiet trails.

In addition to admiring the views, visitors can bird-watch, snowshoe, ski, and even ride horses through the over 50 miles of trails in the park. There are also many historical buildings and homes visitors can tour and enjoy. With over 15,000 acres of diverse land and activities, there truly is something for everyone in Indiana Dunes National Park.

Ecosystem

Indiana Dunes National Park consists of 10 different habitats: prairie, dune, swale, river, swamp, lake, bog, forest, savanna, and marsh. The dune habitat is what many visitors associate with the park. The dunes are composed of four dune complexes. The youngest dunes are closest to the shoreline of Lake Michigan, and the oldest dunes are furthest inland. The types of plants that grow on sand dunes are highly specialized to adapt to the shifting sand. Pitcher's thistle, also known as dune thistle, is one such specialized plant. It has one thick root, called a taproot, that can be up to 6 feet long and has gray green leaves nestled amidst spines and silver hairs. After about 2-8 years of growth, the thistle blooms a beautiful white or light pink flower that can be over 40 inches tall.

The Cowles Bog Wetland Complex is another interesting feature of the park. Also known as the Great Marsh, this complex includes swamps, wet prairie, fen bog, and sedge meadow. Currently, there is a major effort under way to restore the Great Marsh to its former glory by filling ditches, removing non-native plants, and plugging man-made channels known as culverts.

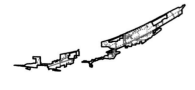

—Park Border — Road ··· Trail

Isle Royale
Michigan

Park History

Throughout history, Isle Royale has been well-known for its copper. Large quantities of copper artifacts dating back to 3000 BC have been found on the island. In the mid-1840s, a copper boom in the state of Michigan was set off by a report from geologist Douglass Houghton. Three separate periods of mining operations rose and fell during the 1800s, with one mining company extracting 95 tons of ore. Once the copper boom wound down, fishing was the main industry for the next several decades.

In the early 20th century, the idea of having a national park in the northern wilderness began to emerge, and in 1931, President Herbert Hoover authorized Congress to find such an area and make the necessary efforts to conserve it. Nine years later, on April 3, 1940, Franklin D. Roosevelt established Isle Royale National Park.

The park consists of a single large island that is surrounded by around 400 smaller islands. In 1981, the island was designated as an International Biosphere Reserve by the United Nations. Even with this added global and scientific significance, the park is the least-visited national park in the contiguous US, receiving only 18,000 tourists per year.

Park Features

The only way to reach Isle Royale is to travel across Lake Superior by boat. This park has 36 campgrounds, each of which is only accessible by foot or boat. Overnight permits are required to camp. The sparse amount of visitors coupled with the isolated nature of the island lend to the feeling of adventure that campers will experience when embarking on their journey to Isle Royale. Be prepared, as it is difficult to leave or contact a ranger should the weather change or something unexpected occur.

Fishing, scuba diving, canoeing, kayaking, and boating are all good activities to capitalize on time spent in the park. Guided boat and ranger tours are popular with those who wish to learn about the various resources of the park. Lake Superior is cold and deep, making it a popular place for experienced scuba divers to explore interesting shipwrecks, take intriguing photos, and challenge their diving skills.

Ecosystem

Isle Royale National Park includes an isolated island surrounded by Lake Superior, along with numerous other lakes and bays. Because animals have to make the difficult trek of at least 14 miles over the frozen lake in the winter, only 18 species of mammals live in the park, including moose, wolves, red foxes, and northern river otters. There are several lakes within the park that contain a small diversity of mussels (four species) which are very abundant. It is estimated that Chickenbone Lake has at least 6.4 million mussels.

The waterways are also populated with many freshwater fish, including the endemic coaster brook trout, found only in Lake Superior. Some other common fish are lake chub, sculpin, and burbot. Scientists are concerned about the fish populations in the area, as the invasive spiny water flea has inhabited the Isle Royale waters. Boreal forests line the bedrock shoreline, including balsam fir, white spruce, paper birch, and aspen, while the interior forests of the park consist of hardwood forests. Sugar maples and yellow birches dominate the interior forests, and in the fall, visitors can see the leaves of these trees change to vibrant colors.

— Park Border

Joshua Tree
California

Park History

The land known today as Joshua Tree National Park has been home to many people groups. The earliest inhabitants of the land were the people of the Pinto culture, who lived there from 8000 to 4000 BC. Not much is known about this group of people. More recent residents of this land include the Serrano, the Cahuilla, the Chemehuevi, and the Mojave. People from all four groups still live in the area around the park today.

Spanish colonists arrived in the area in 1772. The land fell under American control after the Mexican-American War. American settlers soon began raising cattle on the tall grasses in the area. In addition to cattle ranchers, many miners moved into the area to work in the 300 pit mines that were built between the 1860s and 1940s.

As the land became more and more developed, Minerva Hoyt, a Pasadena resident who was passionate about desert plants, became worried about the future of the Mojave Desert and Colorado desert regions. Hoyt, along with other activists, convinced the US government to declare 825,000 acres of land as the Joshua Tree National Monument in 1936. The Joshua Tree National Monument was redesignated as a national park in 1994 under the Desert Protection Act.

Park Features

There are many places to explore in this park. Whether visitors want to camp, hike, or just admire the views, Joshua Tree has over 800,000 acres of land to explore. The Black Rock Canyon is a popular site for campers, hikers, and backpackers due to its beautiful landscape and the Joshua Tree Forest.

Joshua Tree National Park is, of course, most famous for its Joshua trees. The Joshua tree, or Yucca brevifolia, is a sight to behold. The few branches it has are thick and gnarly with prickly needle-like leaves clustered at the top. To 19th-century Mormon immigrants, this tree was reminiscent of the biblical figure Joshua, reaching his arms up to God in prayer. For photographers, landscape painters, and any tree-enthusiasts, Joshua trees are a must-see.

In addition to the Joshua trees, visitors can view a host of other incredible natural features. The park is home to valleys, sand dunes, mountains, oases, and granite monoliths.

Ecosystem

Joshua Tree National Park includes both the Mojave and Colorado Desert, which are home to many endemic plants, such as the Joshua tree, Parry's saltbush, and Mojave sage. Joshua trees are believed to live for 150 years and have twisted and spindly limbs with spiky leaves. While these trees do not have rings, you can judge its age based on height, as these trees grow 1.5-3 inches per year.

Due to the numerous faults that fall along the park, Joshua Tree has many unique geological features, including oases. Desert fan palms require a lot of water to survive, so these year-round oases provide the perfect water supply for these trees and for animals living in the park.

There are many mammals documented in this park, such as squirrels, rats, jackrabbits, and desert kit foxes; most are nocturnal or small to combat the heat. Although 250 species of birds have been documented in the park, it is not surprising that only 78 nest and raise their young in the hot and harsh environment. These hardy birds include the red-tailed hawk, turkey vulture, mourning dove, and great horned owl.

▬ Park Border ▬ Road ··· Trail

Katmai
Alaska

Park History

The first Europeans to arrive in the Katmai park area were Russian fur traders, who came to trade furs with the Alutiiq and other inhabitants of the region. After the now infamous Novarupta-Katmai eruption in 1912, local residents fled the area to escape the devastation wrought by the volcano. They never returned.

Scientists and nature enthusiasts have been interested in the Katmai region for a long time, partially because of its unique geologic features. In 1916, a group sent by the National Geographic Society went to explore the area around Katmai. It was there that they saw something they would never forget: the Valley of Ten Thousand Smokes. This unique geologic feature spurned members of the National Geographic Society and other scientists and naturalists to encourage that the area be protected. In 1918, President Woodrow Wilson designated the area as Katmai National Monument.

The national monument was not very popular among visitors at first, and a ranger wasn't even assigned to the region until 1937. It was not until 1980, with the passing of the Alaska National Interest Lands Conservation Act, that Katmai National Park and Preserve was established. The creation of both a park and a preserve protected the wilderness in the park and permitted the traditional practice of subsistence hunting in the preserve.

Park Feature

Like many of the large national parks in Alaska, it is impossible to run out of things to do on the over 4 million acres of land that make up Katmai National Park. Flightseeing is the best way to really appreciate the dramatic size and diversity of Katmai. From the air, visitors can sometimes spot salmon, bears, moose, and other animals. Backcountry camping and hiking are also popular activities in this park. Lovers of wilderness have no need to worry about running into other tourists when backpacking in Katmai.

By far, the most popular location in Katmai is Brooks Camp. People come from around the globe just to see this part of the park. At Brooks Camp, visitors can spot brown bears and fish and learn about the history of Katmai. Many backcountry expeditions start from Brooks Camp, as do bus tours to the Valley of Ten Thousand Smokes. There are also far more amenities and services at Brooks Camp than in most of the park, offering a visitor center, campground, and ranger-led programs. Regardless of what area of Katmai one chooses to visit, all visitors are encouraged to learn bear and wildlife safety practices.

Ecosystem

Katmai National Park is probably best known for the Aleutian Range, an area with about 14 active volcanoes, making it the world's most active volcanic area. There is a region in the park named the "Valley of Ten Thousand Smokes," so-named because of the volcano Novarupta's pyroclastic flow, or fast-moving volcanic matter, that eventually caused fissures and fumaroles to release steam. Along with the Aleutian Range are the Nushagak-Bristol Bay Lowlands, which contain sand dunes, low ridges, and streams. There are several streams and lakes that are populated with sockeye salmon, a favorite food for Alaskan brown bears. These aquatic regions also contain rainbow trout and lake trout.

Along the Pacific coastline, sea otters, humpback whales, and horned and tufted puffins may be seen. Some year-round residents of the park include ravens, gray jays, and magpies. If visitors plan their visit around June, July, or August, they will see an abundance of wildflowers, including fireweed, northern geranium, Kamchatka lily, and Alaska Indian paintbrush.

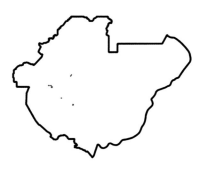

— Park Border ··· Trail

Kenai Fjords
Alaska

Park History

Despite being a land of ice, glaciers, and freezing rivers, the Kenai Peninsula has been a home to humans for centuries. The Sugpiaq, also known as the Alutiiq, lived on the coast of the Kenai Peninsula for over a thousand years. Russian traders arrived at Kenai in the 1780s and 1790s. Many of the Sugpiaq left Kenai Fjords when a permanent Russian Orthodox mission was established in the area in the 1840s.

In the 1970s, many Alaskans and nature enthusiasts proposed that the peninsula be set aside as a National Recreation Area or given some other type of protected designation. In 1973, the Nixon Administration envisioned that Kenai Fjords National Monument would encompass 300,000 acres, sprawling across an ice field and various islands. Unfortunately, the infamous Watergate scandal soon put a halt to those plans.

It wasn't until 1978, under President Carter, that Kenai Fjords was finally secured as a national monument. Shortly thereafter, in 1980, it was re-designated as Kenai Fjords National Park.

Park Features

As the only part of the park to which visitors can drive, Exit Glacier is very popular with hikers. In the winter, Exit Glacier is closed to cars, but it's easy to hop on a shuttle to enjoy some incredible cross-country skiing, snowshoeing, or other winter activities. From the Exit Glacier area, hikers can access the Harding Icefield Trail. It is 8.2 miles round trip and takes between six and eight hours to hike in total. The trail increases in elevation 1,000 feet every mile, so inexperienced hikers may only want to go part of the way up.

Boating is also a popular activity at Kenai Fjords. A good portion of the park is only accessible by water, so a boat tour is a good addition to any visitor's trip. In addition to tour boats, cruise ships leave from Seward Harbor throughout the summer.

Ecosystem

Kenai Fjords National Park is home to almost 40 glaciers in the Harding Icefield. About 51% of the park is covered in ice. These rivers of ice, such as the Resurrection River, contain water supplied from several glaciers and help shape the park by eroding nearby rocks. If visitors leave the bay and head toward Cape Resurrection, they will see a huge, sheer cliff with a bubble-like texture facing the waves. Those "bubbles" create great nesting grounds for birds like black-legged kittiwakes and horned puffins. Other rock formations that can be seen in the park are coves, spires, and arches; the latter two are formed from the erosion caused by wave action.

Along the 545 miles of Pacific Ocean coastline, numerous marine mammals may be seen in the surrounding waters, such as sea otters, Steller sea lions, and numerous species of whales. The seawater from the ocean and the freshwater from glaciers create a unique ecosystem known as an estuary, which lies in a fjord in this park. Within the coniferous forests of the park, Sitka spruce is the most common vegetation. Some of the mammals that roam through these forests include black bears, brown bears, moose, and hoary marmots.

— Park Border — Road ··· Trail

Kobuk Valley
Alaska

Park History

Humans have lived in Kobuk Valley for the past 12,500 years. At least nine different people groups have lived in the valley, including the Akunirmiut, Kuuvaum Kangianirmiut (now known as Kuuvangmiit), and the Inupiaq Eskimos. The Inupiaq people still live there today, hunting caribou across the Kobuk River just like their ancestors did thousands of years before.

Onion Portage, also known as Paatitaaq, has always been instrumental to those living in Kobuk. Onion Portage is a peninsula in Kobuk River, so named because wild onions grow on its banks. This is where the caribou begin their trek across the Kobuk River as part of their biannual migration.

Kobuk Valley was established as a national monument by President Jimmy Carter in 1978. When Carter signed the Alaska National Interest Lands Conservation Act in 1980, Kobuk Valley National Monument was redesignated as Kobuk Valley National Park.

Park Features

Kobuk Valley contains 1.8 million acres of backcountry, making it an incredible trip for anyone who loves adventuring in the great outdoors. Backpacking, camping, hiking, boating, and fishing are all popular visitor activities in the summer. During colder months, those with the proper skills and equipment can also enjoy skiing, snow machining, and even dog mushing.

Given the enormous size of Kobuk Valley, many visitors choose to see it from the sky. Charter plane companies from Kotzebue and Bettles give visitors a chance to see more of Kobuk Valley than they would be able to from the ground.

Another popular sight is the Great Kobuk Sand Dunes. Those traveling by plane can land directly on the sand. Hikers and backpackers love to visit the dunes at different seasons, experiencing warmer weather in the summer and viewing caribou in the fall.

Regardless of what area of the park they visit, visitors are asked to be considerate of those who live near the valley and live off of the land's natural resources.

Ecosystem

Lying north of the Arctic Circle, Kobuk Valley National Park defies expectations. Many would assume that this park is full of snow and ice, but it is actually home to the largest active sand dunes in the Arctic. Along the dunes, visitors can see the Kobuk locoweed, which can only be found on the slopes of the Great Kobuk Sand Dunes.

The tracks of Western Arctic caribou can be seen in dunes, as the largest herd in the US migrates through the park twice a year. In the Kobuk River, which flows through 61 miles of the park, salmon, sheefish, Dolly Varden trout, and graylin can be found inhabiting the waters, in addition to ducks, loons, geese, and swans for a few months of the year.

Along with the Arctic tundra ecosystem, there are boreal forests of birch and spruce, with forest floors covered in moss and caribou lichen. Some of the mammals living in the park include black bears, grizzly bears, wolves, moose, and porcupines. There is only one species of amphibian, the wood frog, that lives in the park. This fascinating animal is able to survive extremely cold temperatures by forming ice crystals and freezing their body.

➤Park Border

Lake Clark
Alaska

Park History

Those not familiar with Alaska may see it as a cold, foreboding place, filled with ice and dangerous animals. However, for thousands of years, the Lake Clark region has served as a home and sustaining source for many people. The Dena'ina, Yup'ik, and Sugpiaq people survived off the land for thousands of years before Russian explorers and prospectors and American settlers arrived.

The Dena'ina still live off the land to this day. When the Alaska Interest Lands Conservation Act was passed in 1980, it made sure that those who sustained themselves on the land, such as the Dena'ina, would still be allowed to fish, hunt, and harvest as they have for thousands of years. Lake Clark, known by Dena'ina as Qizhjeh Vena, "a place where people gather," provides them with salmon, caribou, moose, berries, and other resources. Out of respect for the land that sustains them, the Dena'ina practice sustainable harvesting and hunting, in addition to making sure that they always give some food away to the sick, the eldery, and anyone else who cannot provide for themselves.

Park Features

At 2.6 million acres, there is no shortage of things to do in Lake Clark National Park. Bird-watching, hunting, hiking, camping, rafting, kayaking, and bear-viewing are just some of the things visitors and locals love to do on the grounds of the park.

For those looking to explore the park up close, there are many incredible backpacking trails, such as Low Pass, Trail Creek, and Telaquana. There are no designated campsites or facilities along these trails, so campers will need to prepare thoroughly before deciding whether or not backpacking through the backcountry of Lake Clark is right for them. Popular day hiking locations include Tanalian Falls, Beaver Pond Trail, Tanalian Mountain, and Portage Creek Trail.

Park authorities like to remind visitors to be respectful of any private property they may come across and to avoid crossing into private land. When exploring Lake Clark, visitors must remember that they are traveling through land that others use as their livelihood.

Ecosystem

Lake Clark National Park has a variety of ecosystems, including mountains, salt marshes, forests, and numerous aquatic habitats. While there are over 900 miles of glaciers within the park, most glaciers are in the jagged Chigmit Mountains—part of the larger Aleutian Range.

Along these mountains and the Neacola Mountains, Dall sheep may be seen climbing along the steep, rocky ridges. There are about 123 miles of coast, which includes salt marsh habitats. While this area makes up less than 1% of the park, it is an extremely important habitat for brown and black bears to feed on green sedges after hibernating all winter. The coast also provides a breeding habitat for mallards, Barrow's goldeneyes, and red-throated loons.

The boreal forests consist mainly of white spruce, along with some black spruce and birch. There are numerous lakes and rivers within the park that support over 200,000 spawning sockeye salmon per year. This makes up about 33% of the US catch and about 16% of the total world catch, making it the most productive habitat for these salmon.

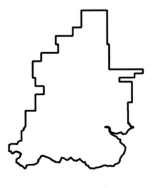

–Park Border

Lassen Volcanic
California

Park History

The Lassen region of Northern California was originally inhabited by several different Native American tribes who used the land primarily as a hunting area. The native people were aware of a large volcano in the area; they spoke of a peak filled with water and fire and expected that it would one day explode. This peak is known today as Lassen Peak, named after Peter Lassen, one of the area's first white settlers.

In the mid-1800s, newspapers from the surrounding area published eyewitness reports of fire being thrown into the sky. In 1859, more witnesses reported eruptions coming from a mountain known as Cinder Cone about 10 miles northeast of Lassen Peak. Despite the activity, the surrounding area was often used as camping grounds, though logging operations infiltrated the region in 1900.

The locals did not approve of the logging and pleaded that the forests be protected. In 1905, President Theodore Roosevelt created the Lassen Peak Forest Reserve in an effort to preserve and restore the area's forests. Two years later, he designated the two prominent volcanoes as national monuments: Lassen Peak National Monument and Cinder Cone National Monument.

In 1915, photographs of an enormous eruption of Lassen Peak spread quickly throughout the country, and the peak became a national sensation. The newly gained attention sparked conversations about turning the area into a national park. A national park bill was introduced in 1915, and President Woodrow Wilson signed it on August 9, 1916, establishing the nation's 10th national park.

The boundaries of the park expanded throughout the 20th century as the park developed. New land was donated to the park by various individuals and corporations. Today, over 500,000 people visit the park every year to explore the serene landscape and see the impressive peaks that overlook it.

Park Features

Standing as the largest plug dome volcano in the world, Lassen Peak is the standout centerpiece of Lassen Volcanic National Park. The peak, reaching a height of 10,457 feet, is the southernmost active volcano in the Cascade Volcanic Arc, which extends from Northern California to British Columbia.

Native Americans who originally inhabited the area took notice of the peak. They knew that it contained "fire and water" and knew that it would one day explode. The peak would remain calm until May 30, 1914. There was a steam explosion that created a crater and a lake on the summit of the volcano. Over the next year, the volcanic activity started to increase, with each proceeding explosion more violent than the last. On May 22, 1915, Lassen Peak exploded in a violent eruption that spewed rock and pumice that landed miles away, with some ash and debris falling as far away as Reno, Nevada. An enormous 30,000-foot column of ash and smoke filled the air and could be seen for 50 miles around. In the area immediately surrounding the peak, the eruption left the landscape burnt and bare, creating what is now known as the Devastated Area.

After this outburst, the volcano only produced minor eruptions and eventually returned to a dormant state in 1921. Since the park's increase in popularity throughout the 20th century, Lassen Peak is visited by hundreds of hikers and climbers every year during the summer. There are several trails that lead to the mountain's summit, as well as several paths that lead tourists to a stunning view of the peak.

Ecosystem

Lassen Volcanic National Park is famous for its volcanic geology. All of the rocks within the park have arisen from volcanoes. Currently, the park contains all four types of volcanoes, which include shield, composite, cinder cone, and plug dome volcanoes. There are also numerous hydrothermal features, such as boiling pools, fumaroles, and mudpots, that can be seen when visiting the park.

While volcanoes are prevalent in the area, visitors can also find lakes, streams, and seasonally wet meadows. The combination of these environments, along with the mixed conifer forest and subalpine zone, allows for a diverse array of organisms to inhabit the park, including over 700 flowering plant species and about 250 vertebrates. Numerous animals live in or around the mixed conifer forests, including black bears, mule deer, mountain chickadees, long-toed salamanders, and several bat species. In seasons of rain, Pacific tree frogs, western terrestrial garter snakes, common snipes, and mountain pocket gophers can be seen in the valleys of wet meadows near the streams and lakes.

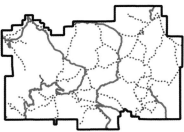

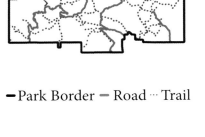

— Park Border — Road ··· Trail

Mammoth Cave
Kentucky

Park History

At 400 square miles, with potentially another 600 miles that remain to be explored, Mammoth Cave is the longest cave system in the world. The deep, dark entrance to Mammoth Cave, hidden under the lush greenery of the surrounding area, has enticed explorers for millennia.

The park's written history begins in the late 18th century, when it was sold by William Pollard to Thomas Lang Jr. No one knows exactly who was the first European to enter the cave system.

In 1838, Franklin Gorin bought Mammoth Cave with the plan of converting it from a mining operation to a tourist attraction. Gorin owned African American slaves and used them to explore the caves and serve as tour guides.

Stephen Bishop, one of Gorin's tour guides, contributed immensely to what we know of the caves today. The visitors he guided described him as intelligent, daring, passionate, and knowledgeable about the caves. He was the first to map the caves and named many of their features, such as Fat Man's Misery, Mammoth Dome, and most famously, the Bottomless Pit.

The Mammoth Cave system and the area around it were designated as a national park in 1941. In 1972, Mammoth Cave was united with the cave system of Flint-Ridge, securing its position as the longest cave system in the world.

Park Features

The Mammoth Cave System is home to hundreds of fascinating geological formations. Visitors to the cave will no doubt be entranced and awed by the spectacularly massive rock formations and the incredibly intricate gypsum flowers.

The most inspiring, or maybe frightening, feature of the Mammoth Cave system is the Bottomless Pit, a 105-foot-deep hole in the ground, discovered by the legendary cave guide Stephen Bishop. The story goes that Bishop was offered a "fistful of money" by a visitor to cross the pit. Supposedly, he placed a ladder across the pit and climbed across, holding a lantern in his teeth. Today, visitors can safely cross the daunting Bottomless Pit over a man-made bridge.

Ecosystem

Mammoth Cave National Park is home to the world's longest cave, with over 412 miles of discovered cave system, in addition to the more than 200 other caves in the park. These caves are rich with life and over 130 species have adapted to these dark environments, like the eyeless cave fish and the endangered Kentucky cave shrimp. About 16 miles of the Green River flow through the cave system, and the other major river is the Nolin River. These aquatic environments are extremely diverse, with about 82 species of fish like bluegill, crappie, yellow perch, and catfish, along with 51 species of mussels.

Besides the cave systems, there are also numerous types of forests in the park that include cedar-oak, oak-hickory, cedar, and pine, to name a few. Prairies occur in small patches of the park where numerous grasses and wildflowers thrive, including bluestem, Indiangrass, goldenrod, and tall coreopsis. Throughout the park, there are about 45 species of mammals such as bats, beavers, pygmy shrews, and white-tailed deer. Birders can see and hear hummingbirds, chickadees, thrushes, and wood warblers, among others.

━ Park Border ━ Road ⋯ Trail

Mesa Verde
Colorado

Park History

For 750 years, from AD 550–1300, Ancestral Puebloans occupied the area that now contains Mesa Verde National Park. There was a great deal of development in culture, agriculture, and architecture during those years. During the last 100 years of the Puebloans, some people left the tops of the mesas and built their houses into the sides of the canyon walls. A severe drought in 1276 drove the Indians out of the area in search of a more sustainable habitat.

Explorers of the late 18th and early 19th centuries recorded seeing the ancient ruins of the Ancestral Puebloans. In 1859, J. S. Newberry made the first known mention of the name Mesa Verde in reference to the surrounding area. Fifteen years later, two white men became the first non-Indians to enter and explore one of the cliff dwellings.

As more and more structures were discovered and explored, concern for their safe-keeping began to arise. In 1886, it was suggested that the area be set aside as a national park, a sentiment that would be repeatedly pushed throughout the next 20 years. From 1901 to 1905, five bills were introduced before Congress to preserve the Mesa Verde area, but none moved forward. In 1906, a bill for the creation of a national park was introduced and passed in June of 1906. President Theodore Roosevelt signed the bill on June 19th.

Excavation and protection of the park began immediately, with trails, roads, exhibits, and park facilities constructed over the next several decades. Today, even as the park recovers from severe wildfire damage, visitation continues to increase with over 500,000 people visiting the park each year.

Park Features

Mesa Verde National Park is known for being the largest archaeological preserve in the US, with over 5,000 sites spread throughout the area. These sites include 600 cliff dwellings, the largest of which is called Cliff Palace. Cliff Palace was built by the Ancestral Puebloans from AD 1190 to 1260 and is known as the largest cliff dwelling in North America.

Cliff Palace was made primarily from sandstone and wooden beams affixed with mortar made from soil, water, and ash. About 150 rooms were built, which are thought to have held approximately 100 people. The size of the doorways throughout the dwelling is often a point of question among visitors. Due to the average human height being 5 feet and 3 inches during the Ancestral Puebloans' time, the doorways are considerably smaller than most modern doorways.

Originally, this cliff dwelling, along with others in the area, was built as a defense against increasingly harsher climate conditions. However, it is thought that Cliff Palace eventually became a site used for social and administrative purposes, perhaps serving as the site of a political state that included surrounding communities.

Ecosystem

There is a slight incline within Mesa Verde National Park that helps form alcoves, or large, arched areas formed in a cliff wall. There are also about 282 seep springs found throughout the park that provide its main source of water, as there are no permanent lakes or streams. The varying elevations of the park allow for numerous ecosystems to exist, such as shrub-steppe communities, mountain shrub communities, and pinyon-juniper forests. Some shrubs seen in the first two communities are sagebrush, rabbitbrush, and cliff fendlerbush. The pinyon-juniper forest is also known as the "pygmy forest" because the trees in that area rarely exceed 30 feet in height.

Among these communities live about 74 species of mammals, including bats, cottontails, mule deer, weasels, and Rocky Mountain elk. Visitors may see eagles, flycatchers, warblers, or sparrows flying through the park as some of the 200 species of birds found in Mesa Verde National Park. There are also numerous reptiles and amphibians found in the park including several species of snakes, lizards, and toads.

━ Park Border ━ Road ⋯ Trail

Mount Rainier
Washington

Park History

In 1792, British explorer Captain George Vancouver named Mount Rainier while on a voyage along the Pacific coast. Throughout the 1800s, dozens of summits of the mountain were recorded. James Longmire kicked off the commercialization of the mountain with the construction of the Longmire Hotel and Health Spa.

In 1888, renowned conservationist John Muir summited the mountain. After the expedition, he began lobbying for conservation of the area. Although most of the mountain was already included in a forest reserve, logging was still allowed, so Muir organized several groups (including the National Geographic Society and the Sierra Club) to advocate for the mountain to be considered for national park status.

The mountain became a national park in 1899 and the area's popularity grew exponentially. Only ten years after its inception, over 30% of the park rangers were needed just for directing traffic in and out of the park. During the Great Depression and World War II eras, visitation fell and infrastructure work increased. This enhanced Mount Rainier's popularity during the rest of the century. Today, the park receives nearly 2 million visitors a year.

Park Features

The best activities and features for visitors to enjoy at Mount Rainier depend on when the visit will take place. During cold months (November to April), the roads beyond the visitor centers are closed. Summertime often finds crowds congesting the small and limited roadways, so trips must be planned wisely. On clear days, Mount Rainier is visible from almost anywhere in the park. However, the weather changes quickly, and clouds and storms can quickly obscure the view. Summiting the mountain is incredibly dangerous and requires significant planning and preparation. At over 14,000 feet, the risk of an avalanche is real, and the minimum party size is restricted to 2 or 3.

During the summer, there are dozens of excellent trails for hiking and backpacking. Those wanting to reach the highest point drivable by car should visit the Sunrise Visitor Center, which sits at 6,400 feet. In the winter, visitors love to snowshoe or cross country ski from Paradise Visitor Center (equipment is available for rental). Sledding is also a favorite for families with younger children. Winter or summer, pictures with the giant old-growth trees are always popular. At nearly 10 feet in diameter, these botanical goliaths are incredible. The park is also popular with birders, as it is the home of both the rare northern spotted owl and marbled murrelet.

Ecosystem

The ecology of Mount Rainier National Park is diverse and extensive. From bears, fish, owls, and boas, to salamanders, mountain goats, pine martens, and bald eagles, the park has it all. This incredible diversity of species is due to extensive precipitation and a large variation in altitude.

There are three distinct ecological zones in Mount Rainier: a forest zone, a subalpine zone, and an alpine zone. Over half the park is a forest zone, and from about 1,700 to 5,000 feet, visitors can find giant Douglas fir trees and ancient cedar groves. At the subalpine zone, endless meadows of wildflowers spotted by hardy pines cover the foothills from around 5,000 to 7,500 feet. Elevations above this are considered beyond the tree line, and small clumps of lichen, mountain heather, and other small biological communities flourish here.

There are 25 major glaciers on Mount Rainier that provide water to the five major river systems in the park. These glaciers and the annual snowpack form numerous waterfalls in the park as well and are best viewed in early summer.

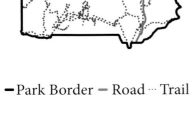

Park Border — Road ··· Trail

New River Gorge
West Virginia

Park History

New River Gorge has been the birthplace of several notable American stories and legends. Nomadic hunter-gatherers roamed the area, living off the land around them. Their descendants are the modern Cherokee and Shawnee people. American settlers began moving into the area in 1755, clashing with the native people in often horrific ways. One of the most famous stories from this era is that of Mary Draper Ingles. During the French and Indian War, Ingles and her sons were taken captive by the Shawnee. The two boys were adopted into the tribe, but Mary Ingles faced a life of servitude. Along with another captive, Ingles escaped and completed an incredible trek of 500 miles over forty days to return to her home and her husband, William Ingles.

Of course, the most famous American associated with New River is the folk hero John Henry. How much of John Henry's story is true and how much is legend no one can say. John Henry was an African American steel driver, tasked with drilling into rock to set explosives that would be used to make way for railroads. Legend goes that John Henry looked industrialization in the face and won, beating a steam powered drill in drilling through Great Bend Tunnel at the cost of his own life.

From Mother Jones, who fought for coal miners, to Carter G. Woodson, known as the Father of Black History, there are many other incredible historical figures who are a part of the tale of New River Gorge. In recognition of both its natural and historical significance, New River Gorge National Park was established in December of 2020, encompassing some of New River Gorge National River, which was established in 1978.

Park Features

New River Gorge is one of the best places in the country to go whitewater rafting. The intensity of a whitewater rafting trip depends on what area of the 53-mile-long New River is visited. The southern part of the river is made of long pools and comparatively easy rapids. This is a popular area for fishing and camping. The northern section of the river is called "the Lower Gorge." This section of the river has massive rapids rushing between and into large boulders. These rapids should only be attempted by experts.

There are many things to do outside of the river of New River Gorge as well. Whether visitors are looking for extreme sports or a relaxing vacation, they won't be disappointed. Camping, hiking, biking, climbing, hunting, and scenic driving are among the most popular activities at the park. There are also many guided and ranger-led activities for kids, families, and anyone interested in learning about the park from the experts who take care of it.

Ecosystem

New River Gorge National Park consists of the New, Gauley, and Bluestone rivers, which make up the New River watershed. The river speed can vary from 3.5 to 7 miles per hour, depending on characteristics like the width of the channel. For hundreds of years, the river has cut through and eroded rock to create the V-shaped gorge and steep valleys of about 900 feet. Within the rivers and streams, there are about 90 different species of fish, including shiner, catfish, and bluntnose minnows. The river has also created numerous rock formations, mainly consisting of sandstone and shale.

The forests of the gorge are dominated by oak and maple, but visitors may also find white pine and hemlock throughout the park. The Appalachian Riverside Flatrock community is a unique environment that contains sedges, cedars, and pines, along with many endemic plants. Visitors may also catch a glimpse of one of the 40 species of reptiles or 50 species of amphibians, such as garter snakes, eastern box turtles, wood frogs, or red spotted newts documented in the park.

— Park Border — Road

North Cascades
Washington

Park History

Thousands of years ago, the Paleo-Indians roamed the valley and surrounding mountains of the current North Cascades National Park area in Washington. When European settlers arrived, the Indian population experienced a considerable decline due to smallpox and other diseases.

The first European to enter the North Cascades area was Alexander Ross. Ross was part of the Pacific Fur Company, which constructed Fort Okanogan in 1811 as the first American settlement in what is now Washington. Fur trappers, white and Native American alike, traded at the fort, with Ross reportedly trading 1,500 beaver pelts in a single season. He began to explore the North Cascades to find a suitable trading route to the coast.

Aside from Ross's expeditions, the area remained largely unexplored until 1853, when Army Captain George B. McClellan led an expedition looking for possible railroad locations. Around this time, prospective miners began panning for gold along the Skagit River. By 1880, little gold had been found and the miners turned to looking for silver and other metals.

The creation of Yellowstone and Yosemite National Parks during the late 1800s led preservationists to argue that more parks should be established. Efforts to create a national park in northern Washington failed to gain approval from Congress and were set aside for decades. In the 1960s, President John F. Kennedy directed the Departments of Agriculture and the Interior to look into creating a national park in the North Cascades. On October 2, 1968, North Cascades National Park was established.

Plans to set aside the majority of the area as wilderness were achieved, as 93% of the park became designated as Stephen Mather Wilderness by 1988, named after the first director of the National Park Service. In keeping with the NPS mandate to preserve and protect natural and cultural resources, hunting, mining, logging, and oil and gas extraction are illegal in the park.

Park Features

One of the biggest highlights of North Cascades National Park is the range after which the park is named. The North Cascades stretch from British Columbia to Northern Washington and are a part of the much larger Cascade Range. These non-volcanic mountains are known for creating dramatic scenery, as well as being a challenge to climb. Both of these characteristics are due to a large amount of precipitation and glaciation, which create a difficult climbing terrain and a rugged snow-capped landscape.

The trails that lead to the mountains are often just as extreme in topography, with steep passes or ridges and an extreme gradient in climate. The most popular time to visit the peaks is from June to September, when it is driest.

Ecosystem

Although there are over 500 lakes and ponds within North Cascades National Park, many are without fish, due to their steep terrain and high elevations. However, the Skagit River supports all five species of salmon and several species of trout for fish enthusiasts. There are a little over 300 glaciers in the park, and some supply fresh water to streams at these higher elevations. Since the park has many aquatic habitats, it comes to no surprise that these ecosystems support about 250 aquatic invertebrates.

Numerous mountains tower over the park, with many exceeding heights of 7,500 feet. In the valleys of the park, forests are abundant with western hemlock, red cedar, and Douglas fir.

About 75 different mammal species live in the park, including elk, bighorn sheep, coyotes, and about 10 species of bats. Birders may see one of more than 200 species of birds that have been documented in the park, including the harlequin duck, pileated woodpecker, marbled murrelet, and the endangered peregrine falcon.

— Park Border — Road ··· Trail

Olympic
Washington

Park History

Olympic National Park is located on Washington State's Olympic Peninsula. For thousands of years, the Olympic Peninsula was home to a variety of Native Americans, such as the Makah people. Native Americans in the northwest region of the United States were so decimated by European diseases that it was not until somewhat recently that the extent of their presence in this region was recognized.

Industry kicked off in the region in the late 1800s. In 1897, President Grover Cleveland established the Olympic Forest Reserve. In 1907, this area was designated as the Olympic National Forest. By the 1920s, so much logging had taken place that outdoor enthusiasts and nearby residents were increasingly dissatisfied with the lack of protection set in place for the beautiful landscape and forests they so enjoyed.

In 1938, Franklin D. Roosevelt responded to the public outcry for increased protection of the area by establishing Olympic National Park. Loggers were displeased with this, and some continued to log in the park illegally. Today, however, no logging takes place within Olympic National Park, and the forests are slowly returning to their former glory.

Park Features

Olympic National Park is popular with backpackers, campers, hikers, boaters, and nature enthusiasts of all kinds. There are five rivers, three lakes, and areas along the Pacific coast that are open to boaters and kayakers dependent on skill levels. Fishing is allowed in the Ozette River, Queets River, Hoh River, and a few other places.

Tidepooling is another popular water activity in the park. Kalaloch Beach 4 and Hole-in-the-Wall are two of the most popular tide pool areas. Visitors of all ages will enjoy spotting marine life such as barnacles, mussels, and other plants and sea creatures.

Uniquely, Olympic National Park provides visitors with the chance to backpack along the beach. Over 95% of Olympic National Park has been designated as wilderness, meaning that hikers and backpackers must be careful to leave no trace and follow National Park Service guidelines.

Ecosystem

From mountains to rain forests, Olympic National Park offers a wide variety of habitats for flora and fauna. Throughout the park, there are five different types of forests that can be found at different elevations, including subalpine, montane, temperate rain forest, lowland, and coastal. Some common vegetation throughout the forests are silver fir, western hemlock, and Douglas fir.

Along the river valleys, otters search for salmon and other freshwater fish swimming in the 10 major rivers within the park, while elk and deer roam these areas. In fact, Olympic National Park has the largest wild population of Roosevelt elk. Besides this rich diversity, the park also includes 73 miles of coastline along the Pacific Ocean, which offers a habitat for a variety of intertidal organisms. Visitors can go tide pooling to see barnacles, seastars, and bull kelp. In fact, large rocks that have visible holes in them were caused by piddock clams that bore into the rock to protect themselves. If visitors look past the tide pools, whales, dolphins, sea otters, or seals may be spotted.

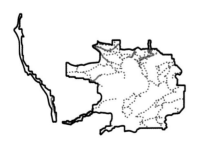

— Park Border — Road ⋯ Trail

Petrified Forest
Arizona

Park History

Archaeological evidence shows that the first permanent communities took hold in what is now the Petrified Forest area of Arizona between 200 and 500 BC. The Ancestral Puebloans constructed apartment-like structures, known as pueblos, in this area during the 1400s AD.

After the United States acquired the southwest, explorers began searching for routes between Spanish colonies along the Rio Grande and on the Pacific coast. Their exploration led them through the northern section of the Petrified Forest in 1853, which they had named Stone Tree Creek. In the 1880s, the Atlantic and Pacific Railroad opened and led to the formation of towns near the Petrified Forest. This, along with other roadways built in the area, increased tourism and commercial interest in the forest during the late 19th century.

Alarmed by the quickly growing tourist population, the Arizona Territorial Legislature asked Congress to preserve the forest as a national park. Their request was not successful, but President Theodore Roosevelt signed the Antiquities Act in 1906, which made the forest a national monument. The government acquired additional land as more trails, roads, and infrastructure were built in the surrounding areas. After much development, the monument became Petrified Forest National Park in 1962.

Today, over 800,000 people visit the park every year to explore the desert and discover ancient petrified "fossil trees."

Park Features

Petrified Forest National Park is best known for exactly what the name suggests: fossils of petrified wood. During the Late Triassic era, downed trees were quickly buried by sediment that contained volcanic ash, which halted the decaying process as the logs were starved of oxygen. Dissolved silicon dioxide from the ash formed crystals inside the wood and slowly replaced all of the organic matter. As the minerals were absorbed, the crystals gradually formed into various colors of quartz, amethyst, and jasper. This process created the petrified wood that the park is named after. The outside of the logs generally retained their original form, even though the logs lost their internal structure during the petrification process.

The majority of the petrified wood found in the park was originally from an extinct type of conifer tree, while others came from extinct *Woodworthia arizonica* and *Schilderia adamancia* trees. The large deposits of petrified wood can be found throughout a 230-square-mile area of the park.

Ecosystem

Petrified Forest National Park has numerous plant and animal fossils that have been discovered within the Chinle Formation. This colorful formation, whose numerous colors are formed from varying layers of sedimentary rocks such as mudstone and silestone, makes up most of the Painted Desert, along with flat-topped mesas and steep buttes. There have been numerous fossils found in the park, some of which date back to the Triassic Period. Visitors will also see lots of petrified wood that are made up of mostly solid quartz and were buried in a river system over 200 million years ago. The coloring of the wood is due to impurities in the quartz.

The two main ecosystems found in the park are the semi-arid grassland and short-grass prairie. Due to the high heat, many animals inhabiting the park are nocturnal. Some animals known to inhabit the area are coyotes, kit foxes, woodrats, spadefoot toads, and western tiger salamanders. Of the 258 bird species documented in the park, many are year-round residents, such as the greater roadrunner, common raven, and horned lark. There is also a variety of cacti, such as the prickly pear and cholla cactus.

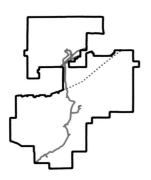

— Park Border — Road ··· Trail

Pinnacles
California

Park History

For thousands of years, the Pinnacles region was inhabited by the people groups known today as the Amah Mutsun Tribal Band and Chalon Indian Nation. They were experts of ecological knowledge and managed and protected the land through traditional techniques such as weeding, selective harvesting, and setting controlled fires. When the Spanish arrived in the 18th century, they brought disease to the region. Many of the Chalon and Amah Mutsun people were either killed by disease or dispersed by the Spanish. The Spanish forced them to speak only Spanish and abandon their cultures, the effects of which their descendants still feel today.

Mexico gained independence from Spain in 1821, transferring the Pinnacles from Spanish to Mexican ownership. California attempted to establish itself as its own country in 1846 but was claimed by the US after the Mexican-American War.

Throughout the late 19th and early 20th century, more and more American homesteaders moved to the region and began to advocate for the protection of the Pinnacles region. Theodore Roosevelt designated the region as the Pinnacles National Monument in 1908. It wasn't until 2012 that Congress passed legislation to redesignate the monument as Pinnacles National Park. The Amah Mutsun Tribal Band and Chalon Indian Nation have also done their part to protect the land that means so much to them, working to restore native plants and traditional methods of ecological management.

Park Features

The feature that often comes up when discussing Pinnacles National Park is, of course, the tall, rocky spires for which the park is named. In addition to Pinnacles' rocks, the fault action in California has created talus caves, which are caves created within rock fragments and boulders at the base of mountains and cliffs. Pinnacles is often seen as a land of extremes, from the tall twisting towers of volcanic rock fragments to the great gashes of the talus caves. Visitors can hike trails that go through the caves up to the rocky pinnacles themselves.

In addition to incredible geologic formations, visitors to Pinnacles can see a host of amazing wildlife. Bird watching is especially popular, with 181 species of birds having been documented at Pinnacles. Perhaps the most coveted sighting is that of the endangered California Condor. Birders have had particular success by hiking toward the rocky spires the park is famous for. Vultures, condors, falcons, and warblers frequently roost atop the spires and monoliths.

Ecosystem

Pinnacles National Park resides near the San Andreas Fault. The ancient movement of the tectonic plates and prehistoric volcanic activity worked together to create the beautiful mountains and rock formations the Pinnacles are so famous for. The rock formations themselves are the remnants of the Neenach Volcano, which caused sections of rock to scatter and slide for miles.

The park has other unique geological features as well, such as the talus caves. The talus caves were also formed by volcanic activity. Boulders rolled down cliffs and lodged themselves into fractures in the ground, forming the narrow cave passageways that visitors can see today. Trails, stairways, and bridges have been built in the caves so that they can be safely traveled through without the need for ropes and ladders.

Pinnacles National Park is also home to a diverse variety of species, ranging from small canyon bats to prowling coyotes, slimy salamanders, and majestic condors. Many of the species that make their home in the pinnacles are species of special concern. The protected status of the park provides these species a safe place to continue to thrive.

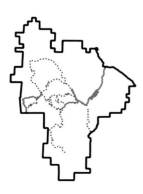

▬Park Border ▬ Road ⋯ Trail

Redwood
California

Park History

Many Native American groups in the Redwood National Park region today have ties back to their ancestors who arrived in the area 3,000 years ago. Their ancestors made use of the redwoods to construct houses and boats.

Before Jedediah Smith explored the area in 1828, no European is recorded as exploring any further inland than the immediate coast. Once gold was discovered along Trinity River in 1850, a secondary gold rush filled the area with hopeful miners, many of whom settled the land after failing to become rich. This led to conflicts with the nearby Native American villages, some of which were forcibly removed or massacred. By 1895, only a third of the Native population remained. The rest died out or assimilated by 1920.

As new settlements were built, extensive logging was needed to maintain building supplies. Concerned citizens and conservationists were alarmed at how quickly the 2-million-acre forest was disappearing, so they sought to preserve the remaining trees. California representative John Raker introduced legislation for the establishment of a national park in 1911, but no action was taken.

In 1918, the Save the Redwoods League was founded by the Boone and Crockett Club to preserve the trees and surrounding land. Due to their efforts and the new state park system, four state parks were founded in the redwood region between 1921 and 1927. The creation of a national park was delayed due to lumber demand during World War II and the following construction boom. After intense lobbying by the Sierra Club, Save the Redwoods League, and National Geographic Society, a bill was signed in 1968 to establish Redwood National Park.

Since the park's creation, over 100,000 acres of land have been added. In an effort to cost-effectively develop the park, some of the original logging roads have been transformed into scenic drives to accommodate the park's 500,000 annual visitors.

Park Features

The redwood trees that fill Redwood National Park are known to reach staggering heights of 240 feet and an impressive diameter of 15 feet. The best and easiest way to experience the majesty of these enormous trees is by taking a trip down Newton B. Drury Scenic Parkway. This 10-mile scenic route takes about 20 minutes to drive and provides a stunning view of thousands of acres of redwood forest. Along the way, visitors can stop at numerous trailheads and head into the forest on foot for a closer look.

Newton B. Drury was instrumental in the preservation of hundreds of thousands of acres of land as parks. Throughout his career, he served as the director of the National Park Service, California State Parks, and the Save the Redwoods League.

Ecosystem

While visitors typically come
to Redwood National Park to
see the world's tallest trees,
many are surprised and amazed
by the numerous habitats
within the park, which aid in
its rich biodiversity. Within the
redwood groves, Douglas firs
can also be found and evidence
of one of the 66 terrestrial
mammals may be seen or heard.
Common mammals inhabiting
the park are different species of
shrews, moles, and squirrels.

While the park has no natural
ponds or lakes, there are
several rivers and streams
populated with salmon and
steelhead. Willows, big leaf
maples, and red alders create
a riparian forest habitat along
the streams where American
dippers, yellow warblers, and
spotted sandpipers have been
documented.

The park also includes prairies
that were once abundant with
grasslands, but more recently,
Douglas firs have started
growing there. Elk and black-
tailed deer are sometimes
spotted in these areas. Another
major area of the park is the
coastline and Pacific Ocean,
which both create numerous
habitats, including tide pools.
Along the shoreline, lucky
visitors may see California sea
lions, harbor seals, gray whales,
or even humpback whales.

━Park Border ━ Road ⋯ Trail

Rocky Mountain
Colorado

Park History

Though almost completely unexplored, the United States acquired what is now Rocky Mountain National Park, along with the rest of the territory included in the Louisiana purchase, in 1803. For many years, Native American tribes called the Rockies home. However, with the advent of railways, extensive homesteading pushed them out by the mid 1800s. A gold rush in 1859 only accelerated Westward expansion across the area.

By 1900, Colorado was an established state, and mountain lodges had popped up throughout the Rocky Mountains. In 1915, President Woodrow Wilson signed an act establishing Rocky Mountain National Park. Tourists flocked to the area before and after World War II. By 1970, large areas of the park had been damaged by overcrowding. Park managers continue to do their best to preserve the unique habitats in Rocky Mountain National Park, as the area receives an annual visitation of over 4 million people.

Park Features

During the 1930s, construction on the Trail Ridge Road was well underway. The intent was to provide an easily navigable and spectacular experience for motor vehicle tourism. Nearly 50 miles long, the road weaves along mountain crests and valleys, providing one of the most scenic drives in America. The experience is a must for anyone wishing to take in the extraordinary beauty of Rocky Mountain National Park. Reaching heights of 12,183 feet, the road features frequent pullouts for unencumbered views.

Along the way, visitors can spot elk, deer, bighorn sheep, mountain goats, marmots, and more. As 11 miles of the road are above the tree line, there is no shortage of views. The Alpine Visitor Center sits at 11,796 feet, overlooking both the east and west halves of the Trail Ridge Road. Here, you can find short walking paths across the peaks for the perfect overlook, exhibits about the various hardy plants that survive the harsh winters, and more. Due to the incredible amounts of snow during the winter time, the Alpine Visitor Center and Trail Ridge Road are both closed from Memorial Day through Columbus Day.

Ecosystem

A large diversity of animals and plants thrive in the valleys of Rocky Mountain National Park. Ponderosa pines, aspens, and dozens of other trees, shrubs, and plants make up the forests of the park. At about 9,000 feet of elevation, the subalpine region emerges, where only coniferous groves and small glacier melt ponds sustain wildlife in this rocky and cold environment. Above 11,000 feet, the ecological zone changes again to what is called an alpine tundra ecosystem. Here, the wind and winter are brutal, so there are rarely any trees. Visitors can spot lichen, cushion plants, tundra, and some small wildflowers growing in these areas.

As for animals, there is no shortage of interesting and resourceful creatures that inhabit the Rockies. Elk are some of the most prevalent creatures, and they move in herds through the valleys and subalpine regions. Smaller mammals like marmots, pikas, bighorn sheep, and more can be sighted by observant visitors. Birders have a lot to enjoy in the park. There are over 270 species of birds that call it home, including ptarmigan, tanagers, nutcrackers, woodpeckers and more.

— Park Border — Road ··· Trail

Saguaro
Arizona

Park History

The imposing saguaro cactus has long been a source of wonder and pride for those who make their home in the Sonoran Desert. The Hohokam people, of what is now modern day Arizona, utilized the saguaro for food and shelter. They also derived much religious significance from the saguaro, particularly its fruit.

Mysteriously, the Hohokam were long gone before the Spaniards arrived in Arizona. Whether they truly disappeared, or their culture simply changed, is a subject of much debate among archaeologists and historians. Regardless, the O'ōdham people proudly consider themselves to be the inheritors of the Hohokam legacy. To this day, the O'ōdham use the fruit of the saguaro to make jelly, candy, and ceremonial wine.

The Spanish settled near the park in 1692 at the San Xavier Mission. Both the Spaniards and the O'ōdham were enemies of the Apache, who frequently raided the region. This back and forth between the European settlers and the Apache continued when Arizona became a part of the US in 1854. Shortly after the US procured the land, the Tucson Mountains became a profitable mining site. Cowboys later joined the miners and started ranches and rangelands on the very land that would later become Saguaro National Park.

In 1933, President Hoover, spurred on by the University of Arizona, dedicated the area as Saguaro National Monument in the Rincon Mountains. Under Kennedy, citizens lobbied for more land to be added to the monument. In 1994, the Tucson Mountain District and Rincon Mountain District were given national park status. Since then, the Saguaro National Park has continued to preserve O'ōdham traditions and expose new generations to the beauty of the saguaro cactus and the surrounding mountain ranges.

Park Features

With over 25 miles of trails and a stunning landscape, the main attractions of Saguaro National Park are hiking, wilderness hiking, backpacking, and camping. There is a diverse range of sites to hike and camp at, such as Manning Camp, which stays at a temperature of 85°F due to its high elevation. There is also the Sky Island Mountain Range, which, despite being in a park famous for its desert flora, can experience up to 6 feet of snow in just 48 hours in the winter. There is also the famous cactus garden, where you can see and learn about the famed saguaro cactus up close.

Saguaro is also a great place to visit for both professional and amateur photographers. The saguaro's silhouette against the mountain ranges and desert sand can form a striking composition. The sunsets in the park, best seen from Gates Pass, Tanque Verde Ridge Trail, and the Javelina Rocks, make for stunning photos no matter who's behind the camera.

Ecosystem

Saguaro National Park spans both the Tucson Mountains and the Rincon Mountains in the Sonoran desert, the only place in the world that can support the saguaro cactus. The mountain ranges were formed by volcanoes that created banded gneiss, striped rock that is prevalent in the Rincon Mountains. The plants that can be found within the park vary with the elevation, with desert scrub communities at the lowest region, followed by desert grassland, oak woodland, pine-oak woodland, pine forest, and mixed conifer forest at the highest elevation in the Rincon Mountains.

The most striking aspect of the ecology of this region is, of course, the famed saguaro cactus. The saguaro, or *Carnegiea gigantea*, can reach heights of over 40 feet tall and can live to be over 150 years old. The root network of a saguaro can span up to 98 feet. The saguaro blossom, the state flower of Arizona, is strikingly white against the muted greens and browns of the surrounding desert. Contrary to the slow-growing and long-living saguaro itself, the blossoms live short but beautiful lives, typically blooming at dusk and wilting by the afternoon of the following day.

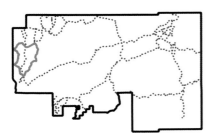

— Park Border — Road ⋯ Trail

Sequoia and Kings Canyon

California

Park History

Although two separate parks, Sequoia and Kings Canyon are jointly overseen and run by the National Parks Service. The giant sequoia forests contained in these two parks span an impressive 202,430 acres and help preserve the southern Sierra Nevada countryside that is displayed in this area.

Sequoia National Park was established on September 25, 1890 as the second national park in the United States. A man by the name of Hale Tharp was one of the first European homesteaders to settle in this area, famously constructing his home out of a hollowed-out fallen giant sequoia tree. In the 1880s, Hale led a battle against the rising logging industry. This fight was finally won, as the logging in the area was promptly ceased with the passing of Sequoia's national park status in 1890.

Kings Canyon, officially incorporated into the National Park System on March 4, 1940, is named after the nearly one-mile-deep glacier-carved valley running through the area. A portion of this park was initially established in 1890 as General Grant National Park in an attempt to halt the widespread clearing of the park's forestry. In 1940, General Grant National Park was greatly expanded and renamed to Kings Canyon National Park.

Both Sequoia and Kings Canyon National Park were created to preserve the magnificent Sierra Nevada landscape from ambitious European settlers of the late 19th century. These two similar parks share a common border and are still managed as one to this day.

Park Features

Sequoia and Kings Canyon are both known for the notable sequoia groves contained within the parks. At Sequoia, Giant Forest is home to five of the ten largest trees in the world. The most well-known of these trees is the General Sherman tree, which boasts the title of largest tree in the world by volume. General Grant Grove, located in Kings Canyon National Park, is connected to the Giant Forest via Generals Highway and is home to impressive trees such as the General Grant sequoia tree.

Although the most popular attractions in the parks are the magnificent sequoia trees, there are still many popular activities to enjoy while visiting Sequoia and Kings Canyon. Visitors enjoy hiking to the various natural wonders around the parks such as Tokopah Falls, Mineral King, Tunnel Log, Moro Rock, and Mt. Whitney (highest point in the contiguous United States). While hiking and backpacking are the most common modes of transportation within the two parks, it is common for visitors to stay in the parks' campgrounds, visit the Giant Forest museum, or venture to the multitude of historical sites scattered throughout the area. There are many sights to see and activities to enjoy for the over 1 million annual visitors to these parks.

Ecosystem

Sequoia and Kings Canyon National Parks have diverse environments among their varying elevations, which range from 1,370 to 14,494 feet. The lowest elevation consists primarily of foothill grasslands, where blue oak woodlands and chaparral shrubs provide shade and hiding spaces for animals like gray foxes, bobcats, skunks, black bears, and numerous species of birds. Visitors can also see groves of the world's largest tree, the giant sequoia, which can live to be over 3,200 years old.

In the upper mountain area, gray squirrels, hermit thrushes, and Wilson's warblers may be seen. The subalpine environment is the highest limit for tree growth; the alpine areas undergo heavy snowfall and high wind speeds, so they contain more rocky, bare areas, along with perennial plants and herbs. Since food is limited in these areas, mammals are less common, but marmots, pikas, and white-tailed jack rabbits live in these higher elevations. Interestingly, most of the lakes and ponds occur at elevations of 8,000 feet or higher. Caves make up another ecosystem in these parks, where visitors can see cave formations, or speleothems, such as towering stalagmites, rimstone pools, and twig-like helictites.

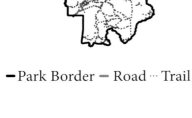

Park Border — Road ··· Trail

Shenandoah
Virginia

Park History

The land contained in present-day Shenandoah National Park was originally a hunting ground, material source, and trading area for Native Americans. In the 1700s, European explorers and hunters moved into the area, settling near springs and streams. Their land and communities greatly developed over the next 150 years, with logging and mining taking place higher in the mountains.

As society flourished and the National Park Service campaigned for more national parks near the East Coast, the idea of a national park in the nearby Appalachian mountain area began to spark some interest. In May 1925, the National Park Service was authorized to acquire between 250,000 and 521,000 acres of land for the new park. However, the legislation stated that the land could not be acquired using federal funds.

Once the Great Depression hit, many of the farming communities were struggling to sustain themselves and willing to sell their land to the government, which added to the private funding for the park. Those who refused to sell their land were evicted and the land was acquired through eminent domain. As the necessary funds were gathered, the park was pieced together and the land was cleared of almost all private housing and infrastructure. On December 26, 1935, Shenandoah National Park was established, and the park currently sees around 1.5 million visitors every year.

Park Features

For a scenic view of Shenandoah National Park, visitors can take a trip down the 105-mile Skyline Drive. This road runs along the ridge of the mountains, taking tourists through the entire park. There are 75 different overlook points that provide views of the Shenandoah Valley and Piedmont. This scenic road is designated as a National Historic Landmark and a National Scenic Byway.

The first recorded plans for the road's construction were made by William C. Gregg, who suggested that a single road be built that would provide drivers with stunning views of the surrounding land. The field surveys for construction began in January 1931, with the official ground-breaking for the road starting in July. The road originally ran for about 20 miles but was extended year after year until it spanned from Front Royal to Blue Ridge Parkway in 1939.

Ecosystem

Shenandoah National Park is the only place that the endangered Shenandoah salamander lives. This park, which is over 95% forested, is abundant with lush chestnut and red oak forests. Visitors can also find maple, birch, basswood, and yellow poplar forests. There are also about 90 small streams, most of which are inhabited by Eastern brook trout. Longnose dace, mottled sculpin, bluehead chub, and fantail darter are also common fish species documented in the park. Besides the streams, there are also wetlands that scientists are currently studying to survey the organisms that inhabit these areas.

While rock outcrops only make up about 2% of the park, these outcroppings are rich with plant species, including 21 state-rare plant species, such as mountain sandwort or three-toothed cinquefoil. Although there are over 50 mammal species within the park, visitors are most likely to see white-tailed deer and gray squirrels. Of the over 190 species of birds commonly seen year-round, residents include tufted titmouse, red-tailed hawks, Carolina chickadees, and barred owls.

➡Park Border ➡ Road ⋯ Trail

Theodore Roosevelt
North Dakota

Park History

Located in the dry badlands of North Dakota, Theodore Roosevelt National Park stands out almost immediately, as it is the only national park in the US directly named after one person.

Today, Theodore Roosevelt is remembered as a rugged outdoorsman with an energetic and boisterous personality. However, this wasn't always the case. Though he had always loved nature and the outdoors, Roosevelt was a sickly child, who found that physical activity helped keep his asthma at bay. As a young man, Roosevelt visited North Dakota, then-called the Dakota Territory, to hunt bison. It was there that he fell in love with the beautiful landscape and the rugged lifestyle of the western United States.

Roosevelt spent a lot of the time in North Dakota, even seeking solace there after the deaths of both his wife and mother. Roosevelt had a love for all things wild. During his presidency, he established the United States Forest Service, created five national parks, and conserved land across the country, establishing national monuments, bird reserves, game preserves, and national forests.

When Roosevelt died in 1919, it was only fitting that land be conserved in his honor. In 1935, the land in North Dakota that Roosevelt so loved was designated the Roosevelt Recreation Demonstration Area. After World War II, this land became the Theodore Roosevelt National Wildlife Refuge. In 1978, the area was recognized for its unique cultural significance and natural beauty, and Theodore Roosevelt National Park was established.

Park Features

Theodore Roosevelt National Park is a wonderful place to visit to take in beautiful landscapes and spot wildlife. The park has 76 miles of scenic drives split across the North Unit and the South Unit and about 100 miles of hiking and backcountry trails to explore on foot or horseback. Backcountry camping is also available, giving visitors a glimpse of what it might have been like to explore and live in the untamed West. Elkhorn Ranch still stands and is open to visitors, so one can truly get an idea of what life was like in the Dakota badlands in the late 19th century.

Visitors to the park have the opportunity to see all the same animals that Roosevelt did. Bison, deer, elk, badgers, bobcats, and longhorns can all be seen at various points along the scenic drives and hiking trails. In the winter, snowshoeing and cross-country skiing are popular visitor activities. Visiting this park is an excellent way to enjoy the history, the beauty, and the wilds of North Dakota.

Ecosystem

There are a variety of ecosystems within Theodore Roosevelt National Park, including grasslands, forests, rivers, streams, and floodplains. The grasslands are the most common habitat in the park and support several species of grass, including saltgrass and western wheatgrass. The grasslands are home to numerous grazing animals, such as wild horses, elk, and prairie dogs.

There are two types of forests that can be seen in the park: juniper woodlands and hardwood forests. The juniper woodlands are a popular place for elk to roam. Juniper berries are an important food source for Townsend's solitaires, cedar waxwings, and American robins. In contrast, the hardwood forests are inhabited by white-tailed deer, porcupines, and numerous birds. Beavers, catfish, minnows, and geese can be seen in or around the Little Missouri River, which flows through the park. The river is the only aquatic environment within the park that can support fish, while the springs and seeps are also used as drinking sources for animals in the park. At times, the river overflows and creates a floodplain environment where cottonwood forests thrive and animals such as bison, deer, and black-capped chickadees roam.

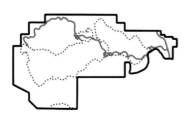

— Park Border — Road ··· Trail

Virgin Islands

U.S. Virgin Islands

Park History

Archaeological discoveries show that as early as 710 BC, groups of Indians migrated from South America and lived on the island of St. John, one of the three Virgin Islands. Centuries later, in AD 100, a population of Taíno Indians inhabited the island. Though Columbus "discovered" the Virgin Islands for Europe in 1493, there were no lasting European settlements there until the Danes settled on St. John after hearing about the promising profitability of cultivating sugar cane.

By 1733, the island was overtaken by cotton and sugar cane plantations, which increased the demand for slaves. Later that year, the slaves revolted, leading a rebellion that would last for several months. The importation of slaves eventually ended in 1802, but the slaves already on the island would not be given freedom until 1848. By this time, the agricultural enterprises had declined considerably, and the plantations were abandoned by 1900.

The United States procured the Virgin Islands in a political move against Germany in 1917. Once word of the islands' beauty made its way to the general public of the US, the National Park Service sparked the idea of establishing a national park. In 1956, Laurance Rockefeller donated the extensive land held by the Jackson Hole Preserve to the NPS. His only condition was that the land had to be protected from any future development. With land and funds acquired, the legislation establishing Virgin Islands National Park was signed by President Dwight D. Eisenhower on August 2, 1956.

The park originally consisted of St. John Island with a management site on St. Thomas, but over 5,500 acres of land were added between 1962 and 1978. Every year, approximately 600,000 people visit the park to snorkel, explore the many beaches, and traverse the subtropical inland trails.

Park Features

A trip to the Virgin Islands National Park makes a great vacation for anyone who loves sand, the sea, and the great outdoors. There are over 20 hiking trails that make for excellent fun for all hikers, especially families.

If water activities are what one is after, the Virgin Islands do not disappoint. At Hawksnest Bay, one can lounge by the beautiful white beach or plunge into the clear blue water and go snorkeling. Hawksnest offers an opportunity to view incredible Elkhorn coral, sponges, and colorful fish. At Cinnamon Bay, visitors can snorkel, windsurf, camp, or simply stroll across the white sand.

Ecosystem

Virgin Islands National Park is made up of terrestrial, coastal, and marine ecosystems that include habitats such as dry-to-moist forests, salt ponds, beaches, mangroves, seagrass beds, and coral reefs. Below the waters of the park, visitors can find over 300 species of fish that make their homes around 50 different species of coral. Some common fish that visitors may see while snorkeling or diving are species of angelfish, butterflyfish, groupers, grunt, filefish, scorpionfish, and the invasive lionfish. If visitors are lucky, they may even see one of the three sea turtle species that visit the area, including the green sea turtle, the hawksbill, and the more rarely seen leatherback turtle.

While many focus on the marine life that inhabits this area, there are also around 144 species of birds, with 35 or so that are permanent residents and others that migrate to the islands at certain times of the year. Some of these birds include hummingbirds, flycatchers, cuckoos, thrashers, moorhens, pelicans, and boobies. However, many of the plants and animals within the park have to compete with nonnative species that several impact the native organisms inhabiting the park.

Park Border ━ Road ⋯ Trail

Voyageurs
Minnesota

Park History

The Northern Minnesota region that contains Voyageurs National Park was originally inhabited by Paleo-Indian groups. The tribes utilized fishing as a major food source.

In 1688, French fur traders, known as voyageurs, explored the area in search of a better source of beaver pelts. The Ojibwe people of the region became suppliers for European explorers, providing fur, food, and canoes throughout the 18th and 19th centuries.

In 1893, gold was discovered along Rainy Lake, sparking a gold rush. Hopeful to strike it rich, miners built a small community to support themselves. However, the boom lasted only five years, and the population soon thinned out.

During the 1880s and 1890s, logging became increasingly extensive, to the point that two major logging companies were created. As trees swiftly disappeared, the Minnesota Legislature of 1891 proposed that a national park be created to preserve the land. However, Congress did not pursue this proposition, and the issue would not be addressed by the government for another 80 years. Legislation establishing Voyageurs National Park was signed by President Richard Nixon in 1971.

The park is most notable for its water resources, drawing the attention of fishermen, canoeists, and kayakers. When the park opened in 1975, there were almost one hundred leased cabins and 120 privately owned homes within the park's boundaries. Since then, the majority of the tenants and their families sold their property and moved away. Today, over 230,000 tourists visit Voyageurs National Park every year.

Park Features

Boating, fishing, kayaking, and canoeing are very popular with Voyageurs' summer visitors due to the large number of lakes and waterways. The park's two tour boats, the Voyageur and the Amik, are both available to rent for school trips, weddings, and other types of gatherings and celebrations. Houseboats are also allowed to stay overnight in the park, with the required permit and reservation.

Hiking and camping are also popular summer activities at Voyageurs. There are some drive-up campsites around the borders of the park for tents, RVs, and car campers. However, all other campsites are accessible only by water, meaning visitors will have to hire a water taxi or take their own watercraft to reach their desired site. Some hiking trails are also only accessible by boat, but there are also many hiking trails that are accessible by car. Many of these hiking trails are closed in the winter, though some are open to cross country skiers or snowshoers in the winter.

Ecosystem

Forests, lakes, and waterways make up the ecosystem of Voyageurs National Park, including areas such as boreal forests, coniferous forests, deciduous forests, wetlands, bogs, and marshes. The four major lakes—Rainy Lake, Kabetogama Lake, Namakan Lake, and Sand Point Lake—make up 40% of the park, so it comes as no surprise that the main access point to the park is by a waterway. These waters are home to lake trout, lake whitefish, cisco, northern pike, sturgeon, walleye, and yellow perch. Visitors may also see common loons and mallards diving for prey in one of the lakes or beavers chopping down wood to create dams.

Voyageurs National Park is one of the few national parks in the lower 48 states where visitors have a chance of seeing a moose, as the boreal forest is a great habitat for these animals. Bird enthusiasts flock to the park for a chance to see the highest density of breeding warblers in North America. Visitors can also see chickadees, thrushes, vultures, owls, sandpipers, herons, gulls, common loons, and the bald eagle, a year-round resident.

━Park Border ━ Road ⋯ Trail

White Sands
New Mexico

Park History

People have inhabited the Tularosa basin, the location of White Sands National Park, for thousands of years. A look back through time at the lives of these early inhabitants would display a world full of mammoths, giant sloths, and bison, as well as people who had developed incredibly effective stone tools and weapons.

After these Paleolithic people had long since come and gone, the Apache moved into the Tularosa Basin. They lived in wickiups and teepees and frequently roamed the basin to hunt and gather. When European explorers arrived, they found that the Apache weren't going to leave their homeland without a fight. The famous Apache leaders, Victorio and Geronimo, led their people to war against the American Buffalo Soldiers. The Apache Wars, as they are called today, were at their peak from 1849 to 1866, though small skirmishes between the Apache and the US continued until 1924, when the Apache were forcefully moved from the Tularosa Basin to the Mescalero Apache Indian Reservation, where their descendants still live today.

As the Apache wars came to an end, the Tularosa Basin became largely populated by cattle ranchers and homesteaders. White Sands National Monument was designated in 1933, shutting down some of the industrialization that had begun to flourish in the basin. In 1945, the area of Tularosa Basin around the national monument was used as a missile test site. The White Sands Missile Range surrounds the national park to this day. In 2019, President Donald Trump signed a bill that designated the national monument as White Sands National Park. The bill also transferred some land from the national park to the missile range and vice versa, adding a net total of over 2,000 acres of land to the park.

Park Features

With around 600,000 visitors per year, White Sands National Park is the one of most visited protected sites in New Mexico. The main attraction of this park is, of course, the beautiful white gypsum sand dunes for which it is named. Dunes Drive, an 8-mile road through the dunefield, provides drivers with the chance to see miles of gypsum dunes. Bike riders can also take advantage of this road, which goes by hiking trails, picnic areas, and outdoor exhibits.

There are five hiking trails in White Sands, totaling about 9 miles, including a 0.4-mile boardwalk that is completely wheelchair- and stroller-accessible. In addition to making for great hiking trailers, some of the dunes can be used for sledding, a popular activity among guests.

Ecosystem

White Sands National Park includes a basin surrounded by gypsum-containing mountains, including two mountain ranges: the San Andres Mountains and Sacramento Mountains. Rainfall and snowmelt help bring gypsum from the mountains to the basin floor, which helps form the world's largest gypsum dunefield. New dunes are formed from Lake Lucero, which contains a lot of gypsum-laden water and selenite crystals in the mud. Wind transports these crystals and breaks them down to form sand seen on dunes. The spaces between sand dunes are known as interdunal flats. In these areas, visitors can see wildflowers, grasses, and small trees and shrubs like Colorado four o'clock, Indian ricegrass, and desert willow.

To adapt to the pale environment, there are many white species of animals, such as the Apache pocket mouse, bleached earless lizard, and sand-treader camel cricket. In some of the springs and creeks, like Malpais Spring or Salt Creek, visitors may catch glimpses of the endemic and threatened White Sands pupfish. The park also includes the northern part of the Chihuahuan Desert, so in brushy areas of the park, cacti like cane cholla and desert spoon may be seen.

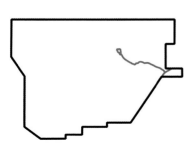

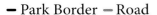

— Park Border — Road

Wind Cave
South Dakota

Park History

The land of Wind Cave National Park was inhabited by the Lakota Indian tribe before the 19th century. The Lakota Indians believed the cave itself was sacred, a hole in the ground that blew air, where their ancestors first emerged from the underworld. It is widely believed that no one ever entered the cave due to its sacredness.

In 1881, as sibling explorers Tom and Jesse Bingham were traversing Southwestern South Dakota, they heard wind coming from a nearby 10-inch hole in the ground. After further inspection, they determined that the hole led to an enormous cave. Entry into the cave later that year revealed a 44-square-mile expanse of passageways surrounded by boxwork and frostwork calcite formations. In 1890, the South Dakota Mining Company attempted to find valuable minerals in the cave but was unsuccessful, so Jesse McDonald, the overseer of the mining company, developed the area for tourism.

The cave was named Wind Cave because the passages were said to "breathe" as air traveled in and out. As word spread, curious visitors began to arrive. In 1893, the McDonalds formed the Wonderful Wind Cave Company with John Stabler. The relationship between Stabler and the McDonalds quickly turned sour, with concerns reaching the Department of the Interior. It was decided that the land did not rightfully belong to either party, and the land was soon placed under federal government protection.

In 1903, President Theodore Roosevelt established the cave and surrounding areas as Wind Cave National Park. This was the first cave in the world to achieve national park status. With cave tours starting at $0.50, tourists came in droves to experience the breathing passages. Since then, visitation has increased to over 650,000 people per year, and new reaches of the cave are continuing to be explored and mapped every year.

Park Features

As visitors explore the middle and lower levels of Wind Cave, they'll see a curious formation of rock along the walls and ceiling of the passages. With a strange, web-like appearance, these thin blades of calcite are collectively known as boxwork, the origins of which remain one of the biggest mysteries of the cave. Boxwork forms when calcium carbonate dissolves and then crystallizes inside cracks in the surrounding rock. As the surrounding rock erodes, the honeycomb-shaped blades of calcite are left protruding from the rock. The boxwork found in Wind Cave is more abundant and well-formed than any other cave system in the world.

Ecosystem

Wind Cave National Park is home to one of the longest caves in the world, spanning roughly 149 miles. This is one of the few places visitors can observe boxwork. Parts of the cave are dated over 300 million years old, making it one of the oldest caves in the world. One of the current battles for the park is a disease known as white-nose syndrome, which has been impacting their bat species since 2019.

Outside of the cave, there are two main ecosystems that make up the park: the prairie grasslands and the forested hillsides. The park is mainly open prairie with varying types of grass, depending on the amount of rain that specific area receives. Visitors may have the highest chance of seeing elk, bison, or deer along the ecotone, where the central mixed grass prairies blend into the forested hillsides. Compared to the prairie, the hillsides are higher in elevation, cooler, and wetter. The forests include cottonwood, bur oak, and ponderosa pine. Flying along or above the tree line, visitors may see the American kestrel, Cooper's hawk, killdeers, and mourning doves.

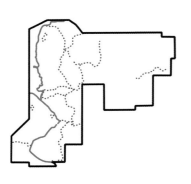

— Park Border — Road ··· Trail

Wrangell-St. Elias
Alaska

Park History

At 13.2 million acres, Wrangell-St. Elias Park and Preserve is bigger than many countries, including Denmark, Costa Rica, and Switzerland, and is the largest national park in the US. Like many Alaskan National Parks, Wrangell-St. Elias was established with the passing of the Alaska National Interest Lands Conservation Act in 1980.

Before it was a national park, Wrangell-St. Elias was a vast swath of unknown wilderness, ice fields, glaciers, and mountains. The Ahtna, Upper Tanana Athabascans, Eyak, and Tlingit peoples lived in various places throughout the park and along the coast. The first Europeans to arrive in the region were Russians, who sought to explore and gather resources to trade. After violent conflicts with the Native Alaskans, the Russians seemed to have halted in their efforts to explore the Copper Basin region near the Wrangell mountains.

The United States acquired Alaska in 1867, and American settlement in the region boomed in the 1890s with the Yukon gold rush. In addition to the discovery of gold, many other ore and mineral deposits were discovered in the region. The Kennecott mines took full advantage of this, mining silver ore and copper. The mining prospects in Alaska spurred the creation of massive railroads and boomtowns. Eventually, the Americans had mined all they could, and the Kennecott mines and railroad were shut down in 1938.

Park Features

Given that visitors have over 13 million acres of land to explore, it's easy to imagine that there is something for everyone at Wrangell-St. Elias. Uniquely, sport hunting is allowed at Wrangell-St. Elias, as it is at other Alaskan national preserves, due to the Alaska National Interest Lands Conservation Act. Bison, caribou, black bears, wolves, and muskox are just some of the large game that can be hunted by a select few park visitors. Hunters must be awarded a permit to hunt different species, such as bison. For bison specifically, roughly 100 permits are handed out each year, depending on the health and size of the herds.

One would be amiss to visit Wrangell-St. Elias without taking advantage of the beautiful trails or backcountry hiking opportunities. In addition to day hiking and backpacking, visitors to this park also have the opportunity to go mountaineering. Attempting to summit the peaks of the Wrangell or St. Elias mountains requires a permit from the proper authorities and a wide array of equipment and technical knowledge. Summiting these mountains involves climbing glaciers and dealing with intense conditions, so climbing these mountains should not be attempted without experience or a knowledgeable guide.

Ecosystem

Wrangell-St. Elias National Park contains diverse landscapes, including volcanoes, glaciers, rivers, and forests. Mount Wrangell is one of the largest (by volume) active volcanoes in the world. The glacial system dominates about 35% of the park and contains one of the nation's largest glacial systems, along with Hubbard Glacier, North America's largest tidewater glacier. These glaciers provide water and sediment to glacial streams, which eventually trickle down to larger rivers, such as the Copper River. Salmon, rainbow trout, and northern pike can be found in some of the rivers and streams.

The forest ecosystem is considered a boreal forest and is full of spruce trees, paper birch, aspen groves, and numerous sedges. A large diversity of birds live in the park. For some birds, Wrangell-St. Elias is just a stop on their long migratory journey, while for others, it is their permanent home. Visitors can help park rangers by being a part of the annual Christmas Bird Count that takes place from December 14 to January 5 to document species such as chickadees, redpolls, gray jays, and pine grosbeaks.

Park Border Road Trail

Yellowstone
Idaho/Montana/Wyoming

Park History

The area that encompasses Yellowstone National Park was first explored by European Americans in the early 1800s, and the first organized expedition of the area was assembled in 1870. The next year, Ferdinand V. Hayden explored the area and quickly became its most enthusiastic advocate, urging the government to "set aside the area as a pleasure ground for the benefit and enjoyment of the people." Ulysses S. Grant signed the Act of Dedication in 1872, which would make Yellowstone the first national park in the US, and arguably the first national park in the world.

By 1915, the number of automobiles entering the park was climbing to the thousands, and horse travel on roads was prohibited to avoid conflict between automobiles and horse-drawn carriages.

After World War II, visitation increased tremendously, which prompted park officials to implement Mission 66. Mission 66 was a 10-year program aimed at modernizing and expanding the park service facilities. The traditional log-cabin-style construction was traded in for a more modern style. There was a resurgence of the older traditional style in the 1980s, but enormous forest fires in 1988 took advantage of the traditional wooden designs, prompting the structures to be rebuilt with a modern design.

In 1995, there was the famous Yellowstone Wolf project. The last wolf had been killed in 1926, and the project aimed to bring wolves back to Yellowstone. The restoration was a way to manage the rising elk population, which gave biologists the opportunity to study the effects of a top predator returning to an ecosystem. There are now considered to be over 120 wolves in the park.

Park Features

One of the standout features of Yellowstone that inspired the park's establishment is the geyser known as Old Faithful. This thermal wonder was discovered in 1870 by the Washburn Expedition. Members of the expedition noticed that the geyser "faithfully" erupted at regular intervals and named it accordingly.

Old Faithful is located in the Upper Geyser Basin in the southwest section of the park. Visitors can watch the geyser's eruptions from the geyser-viewing area, one of the most visitor-friendly and accessible areas of the park.

The eruptions, on average, reach heights of 130 to 140 feet and generally last 1.5 to 5 minutes. Each eruption spews out between 3,700 and 8,400 gallons of boiling hot water measured at around 200°F.

Predicting Old Faithful's eruptions (20 per day) can be done with remarkable accuracy, often being predicted at a 90% confidence rate based on the previous eruption with only a 10-minute variation. These predictions are maintained and recorded by the staff at the park using a very simple technique—observing the geyser, timing with a stopwatch, and writing their observations in a logbook.

Ecosystem

Yellowstone National Park contains more than 10,000 hydrothermal features, such as hot springs, mudpots, fumaroles, and half of the world's active geysers. There are several extremophiles that inhabit the hot environments, also known as thermophiles, including thermophilic archaea, cyanobacteria, and eukarya such as algae and protozoans.

Numerous volcanic eruptions have occurred, including three super eruptions, with one erupting and forming the Yellowstone caldera. This crater is roughly 30 by 45 miles wide, and the volcanic rhyolites and tufts that make up the caldera are rich in quartz and potassium feldspar.

Yellowstone National Park forms the core of the Greater Yellowstone Ecosystem, which is one of the largest temperate-zone ecosystems on Earth. The winters include short days and lots of snow, so organisms that live in this area must be adaptable to these harsh conditions to survive. For example, some animals use the hydrothermal areas or live beneath the snow to keep warm. The park has one of the largest elk herds in North America and the largest free-roaming, wild herd of bison in the United States.

─ Park Border ─ Road ⋯ Trail

Yosemite
California

Park History

Native Americans were the main residents of the Yosemite Valley until the gold rush of 1849 lured settlers to California's Sierra Nevada mountain range. Tourists followed the gold rush, and exploitation of the valley began. To prevent further damage to the ecosystem of the area, President Lincoln signed The Yosemite Land Grant, which designated the Yosemite Valley and Mariposa Grove a public trust of the state of California. This was the first time that the United States government had protected land because of its natural beauty for the enjoyment of the people. Although this action led to the eventual development of the National Park System, Yosemite was not the first national park; it was the third. Yellowstone National Park was created in 1872 and Sequoia National Park in 1890, one week before Yosemite.

John Muir, the famous environmental trailblazer, was troubled by the destruction of forests and meadows surrounding the Yosemite Valley and campaigned for the protection of the region. In 1890, Yosemite National Park was created by congressional action and signed into law by President Benjamin Harrison; however, the Yosemite Valley and Mariposa Grove lands already granted to the state of California were not included. In 1903, President Theodore Roosevelt traveled to California and went camping with Muir. Muir persuaded Roosevelt and state authorities that the national park needed to be expanded to include the Yosemite Grant. In 1906, the president signed a law returning Yosemite Valley and Mariposa Grove to the federal government.

Yosemite is one of the most visited national parks in the US, with four to five million visitors each year, the majority of whom come to the park May through October.

Park Features

Yosemite National Park covers an area of nearly 12,000 square miles, but most visitors only visit the 6 square miles of Yosemite Valley where the most recognized landmark of Yosemite, Half Dome, can be found.

Half Dome is a granite dome rising 5,000 feet above the valley floor, with an elevation of 8,846 feet. The name comes from its shape, which looks like a dome cut in half with three smooth and round sides and one side that is a sheer face. In 1865, a California Geological Survey report declared that Half Dome was "perfectly inaccessible, being probably the only one of the prominent points about the Yosemite which never has been, and never will be, trodden by human foot." Despite this claim, the summit was reached in 1875 by George Anderson. Today, approximately 50,000 hikers reach the summit of Half Dome each year. They use metal cables to climb the last 400 feet to the summit. Less ambitious visitors can admire this Yosemite icon from various locations in the park. Mirror Lake, at the base of Half Dome, provides a great perspective of the sheer size of the stone monolith. Washburn Point and Glacier Point also provide awe-inspiring views of Half Dome.

Ecosystem

The large elevation range (1,800 to 13,000 feet) of Yosemite allows for a large diversity of vegetation and wildlife. Native fish, including the California roach, Sacramento pikeminnow, and riffle sculpin, are only found in the lower elevations of the park. However, do not be surprised if you see or catch trout, as they are the most common non-native fish introduced to the park.

The lower forests include chamise, blue oak, interior live oak, and gray pine. In this ecosystem, black bears may be seen feasting on berries in the spring or summer from the manzanitas that also bloom in this area. The tree-dwelling Pacific fishers use hollows of pine and fir as their home in this region. This zone also consists of giant sequoia groves that scientists believe may be a potential roosting habitat for bats that live in the park. The next elevation region is called the upper montane forest, while the two highest regions are the subalpine and alpine forest. Both include cooler climates with long, cold, and snowy winters. While this environment sounds harsh, the Sierra Nevada bighorn sheep and Sierra Nevada red fox inhabit these areas.

━ Park Border ━ Road ··· Trail

Zion
Utah

Park History

Archaeology reveals a long history of human settlement in the Zion region. Regular flooding and ideal elevation ranges allowed for fertile soil and abundant vegetation growth, which drew animals and hunters. The first documented people to settle in the region were the Paiute people, who thrived in the ideal farming and hunting conditions. In the early 19th century, the first Western settlers—Mormons from the East Coast—made their home in the area. Shortly thereafter, explorer John Wesley Powell visited and made notes about Zion's beauty and geological features. Just a few years later, the area was further explored and mapped by George Wheeler and G. K. Gilbert.

In the early 20th century, Utah had become increasingly accessible with the advent of railways. It was not long before artists found inspiration in Zion valley. Paintings by Frederick S. Dellenbaugh were featured at the Saint Louis World's Fair in 1904, spurring additional travel to the area. In 1919, President Taft made Zion the 15th national park. The Union Pacific Railroad soon constructed a lodge in the valley, beside the Virgin River.

Travel in and out of the canyon was not simple, as the 1,000-foot sheer cliff faces made it nearly impossible to travel down safely. It was for this reason that lawmakers at the national and state levels appropriated funds to construct the Zion-Mount Carmel Highway and Tunnel. For over three years, workers struggled to bring the 25-mile design to life. The most difficult challenge was the 1.1-mile tunnel straight through the mountains. Through a combination of drilling and blasting, the road was finally completed in 1930, making the park even more automobile-friendly.

Today, roads and trails crisscross Zion, making exploration easy and enjoyable for the over 4 million annual visitors the park receives.

Park Features

Zion is full of incredible views and activities. One such activity that is popular with visitors is hiking to Angels Landing. The beautiful views from the top of Angels Landing are hard-earned. In under five miles, hikers gain over 1,600 feet of elevation—much of this on cliff-face switchbacks affectionately called Walter's Wiggles. After that, the danger increases as the trail narrows, and the only support comes from chains bolted into the rock. Over a dozen people have died on this hike, and although it's a favorite of many, the faint of heart should take note, especially in the summertime, as heat indexes reach well over 100°F.

Another visitor favorite is the Narrows, named for the 14-mile channel of rock through which the Virgin River flows into the canyon. Those wishing to tackle this adventure should be ready to wake up early and get their feet wet. The water is lowest from late spring through summer but still chilly, so many people will opt to rent waders from an outfitter in town the night before. Once inside the canyon, visitors are often awestruck by the rock walls that rise hundreds of feet on either side, reflecting brilliant hues of red, orange, and yellow as the sun rises.

A more family-friendly favorite is the Weeping Rock. Even though it is the shortest trail in the park, it is still worth the time for hikers of all skill levels. Hanging gardens drape around the cliff, which has been hollowed out by centuries of water flow. Depending on the time of year, a fine mist or fully fledged waterfall can greet guests at the end of the half-quarter-mile trail—a welcomed blessing in the summer months.

Ecosystem

Zion is renowned for its iconic, layered canyon rock formations and monolithic mountains. Much of this has resulted from sedimentation, lithification, uplift, and erosion. The oldest volcano in the park, Kolob Volcano, has erupted several times in the last million years The iconic canyon was formed by a landslide that damned the Virgin River. The Virgin River makes the valley a lush riparian area and is the main source of water for organisms in the park. As such, it is common to spot willows, cattails, rushes, and other aquatic plants. At higher elevations, away from running water, visitors find juniper trees and ponderosa pine forests, while on the plateaus, pines, firs, and aspens flourish.

The list of animals that call Zion home might as well be endless. While visiting the park, don't forget to look up and try and catch a glimpse of one of the 291 species of birds that have been documented in Zion. Among the mammal populations are bighorn sheep, mule deer, foxes, rock squirrels, ringtails, and more. During the evenings is when most mammal species are active. Zion is also a great place to view the night sky and stargaze, as it has been certified as an International Dark Sky Park.

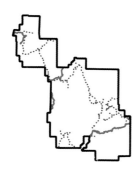

—Park Border — Road ··· Trail

Photo Credits

Cover – Aniket Deole; 1 – Benjamin Rascoe, Suraj Gattani; 2 – Robert Koorenny; 3-4 – Rachel C; 5 – NPS Photo, NPS Photo; 6 – NPS Photo; 7-8 – NPS Photo; 9 – Jake Nackos, NOAA; 10 – Ashley Knedler; 11-12 – NOAA; 13 – Tevin Trinh, Stephen Pedersen; 14 – Drew Darby; 15-16 – Brian Miller; 17 – Scott Van Hoy, Chase McBride; 18 – Mick Haupt; 19-20 – Mick Haupt; 21 – Catholic 85/Wikipedia, NPS Photo/A. Bourque; 22 – NPS Photo/Heriberto Irizarry; 23-24 – Evan R; 25 – Dustin Weist, Ken Lund/Flickr; 26 – Vincent Ledvina; 27-28 – Rich Martell; 29 – Jeremy Gallman, Donald Giannatti; 30 – Agnieszka Mordaunt; 31-32 – Oleg Chursin; 33 – Patrick Hendry, Ganapathy Kumar; 34 – Caitlyn Noble; 35-36 – Caroline Dinouard; 37 – Evan Sanchez, NPS Photo/Chris Roundtree; 38 – Doran Erickson; 39-40 – NPS Photo/Evan Lovell; 41 – Matt Noble, NPS Photo/Peter Jones; 42 – NPS Photo/Peter Jones; 43-44 – Matt Noble; 45 – NPS Photo/ Susanna Pershern, Priya Karkare; 46 – Jeremy Bishop; 47-48 – Priya Karkare; 49 – Clay Banks, NPS Photo; 50 – Leslie Cross; 51-52 – Leslie Cross; 53 – Dimitar Tantchev, Evan Smogor; 54 – Jenn Wood; 55-56 – Anukrati Omar; 57 – Benjamin Lehman, NPS Photo; 58 – NPS Photo; 59-60 – Travis Essinger; 61 – Meric Dagli, Casey Horner; 63-64 – Jeremy Bishop; 65 – Paul Van Lake, Joris Beugels; 66 – Jesse Brack; 67-68 – Hari Nandakumar; 69 – Alec Douglas, NPS Photo; 71-72 – Bryan Goff; 73 – NPS Photo/R. Cammauf, NPS Photo/R. Cammauf; 74 – Morgane Perraud; 75-76 – Mark Jacquez; 77 – NPS Photo/DevDharm Khalsa, NPS Photo/Sean Tevebaugh; 78 – NPS Photo/Sean Tevebaugh; 79-80 – NPS Photo/Sean Tevebaugh; 81 – Intricate Explorer, Logan Troxell; 82 – Keran Yang; 83-84 – Chris Hardy; 85 – Matt Noble, Matt Noble; 86 – Matt Noble; 87-88 – NPS Photo/Tim Rains; 89 – Marc Meyer, Matt Howard; 90 – Davina Schaetz; 91-92 – Brad Stallcup; 93 – Matt Noble, Matt Noble; 94 – Omer Salom; 95-96 – Matt Noble; 97 – Aleesha Wood, Nick Dunlap; 98 – Sean Pierce; 99-100 – Andreea Chidu; 101 – NPS Photo, NPS Photo; 102 – NPS Photo; 103-104 – Donald Giannatti; 105 – Alex Perz, Matt Noble; 106 – Jeremy Vessey; 107-108 – Matt Noble; 109 – Chad Madden, Sarthak Navjivan; 110 – Ivana Cajina; 111-112 – Robert Thiemann; 113 – Leonardo Corral, Eric Dekker; 114 – Brandon Frie; 115-116 – Vince Rankin; 117 – Jelle de Gier, Rina Miele; 118 – Anton Repponen; 119-120 – NOAA; 121 – NPS Photo, Merry; 122 – Ben Klea; 123-124 – USGS Photo; 125 – NPS Photo/Mitch Smith, NPS Photo; 126 – NPS Photo/HABS; 127-128 – NPS Photo/Mitch Smith; 129 – NPS Photo, NPS Photo; 130 – NPS Photo; 131-132 – Adam Bouse; 133 – Ray Dumas, Joe Ross; 134 – Hans Isaacson; 135-136 – Ray Dumas; 137 – Brent Cox, Elliott Engelmann; 138 – Eleonora Patricola; 139-140 – Alessandro Rossi; 141 – NPS Photo, Paxson Woelber; 142 – Jeremy Bishop; 143-144 – Jeremy Bishop; 145 Jonathan Wheeler, Phillip Sauerbeck; 146 – Clemente Cardenas; 147-148 – Daniel H Tong; 149 – NPS Photo, NPS Photo/Eileen Devinney; 150 – NPS Photo; 151-152 – NPS Photo; 153 – NPS Photo/A. Miller, NPS Photo/K. Lewandowski; 154 – NPS Photo/K. Lewandowski; 155-156 – NPS Photo/K. Miller; 157 – Stephen Leonardi; 158 – Anna French; 159-160 – Priya Karkare; 161 – NPS Photo, L. Allen Brewer; 162 – NPS Photo; 163-164 – NPS Photo; 165 – Alec Krum, NPS Photo; 166 – Alec Krum; 167-168 – Alec Krum; 169 – Nathan Dumlao, Ryan Stone; 170 – Jordan Steranka; 171-172 – Gilbran Hamdan; 173 – NPS Photo/Dave Bieri, NPS Photo/Gary Hartley; 174 – NPS Photo/Gary Hartley; 175-176 – NPS Photo/Gary Hartley; 177 – Justin Cron; 178 – Zoe Reeve; 179-180 – Nate Foong; 181 – Yux Xiang, Katie Moum; 182 – Ben Eubank; 183-184 – Nate Foong; 185 – Mason B, John Fowler; 186 – NPS Photo/Hallie Larsen; 187-188 – NPS Photo/ Andrew V Kearns; 189 – NPS Photo/Kurt Moses, NPS Photo/Emily Novack; 190 – SAIRA; 191-192 – NPS Photo; 193 – Hasmik Ghazaryan Olson; 194 – Zelong Li; 195-196 – Elizabeth Explores; 197 – Ivan Zhirnov, NPS Photo/NH; 198 – Andrew Gloor; 199-200 – Carlos Fox; 201 – Frankie Lopez; 202 – Karl Magnuson; 203-204 – Robert Murray; 205 – Ross Stone, James Fitzgerald; 206 – Anagha Varrier; 207-208 – Vladimir Kudinov; 209 – NPS Photo/Neal Lewis, andrew-neel-unsplash; 210 – taylor-wright-unsplash; 211-212 – NPS Photo/Neal Lewis; 213 – Jason Rojas, Jeff Dewitt; 214 – Jeff Dewitt; 215-216 – NPS Photo/Dave Bruner; 217 – Josh Duncan, Roger Darnell; 218 – Hans Isaacson; 219-220 – Everett Carrico; 221 – Ed Lombard, NPS Photo; 222 – Yinan Chen; 223-224 – NPS Photo/Dimse; 225 – Ben Soyka, Ben Soyka; 226 – Madeline Pere; 227-228 – Jeremy Brady; 229 – Sophia Simoes, NPS Photo; 230 – NPS Photo; 231-232 – NPS Photo; 233 – NPS Photo, NPS Photo; 234 – NPS Photo; 235-236 – NPS Photo/Neal Herbert; 237 – Steven Cordes, Miss Mushroom; 238 – Frank OConnor; 239-240 – Anukrati Omar; 241 – Mathieu Olivares; 242 – Johannes Andersson; 243-244 – Aniket Deole; 245 – Alex Azabache; 246 – Aaron Roth; 247-248 – Matthias Mullie; All park outlines derived from NPS.gov and formatted/edited for use by Impressive Inspirations